Unconscious
Wisdom

Unconscious
Wisdom

A Superego Function in Dreams, Conscience, and Inspiration

Dan Merkur

STATE UNIVERSITY OF NEW YORK PRESS

Published by
State University of New York Press, Albany

For information, address State University of New York Press,
90 State Street, Albany, NY 12207

Production by Kelli Williams
Marketing by Anne M. Valentine

Library of Congress Cataloging-in-Publication Data

Merkur, Daniel.
Unconscious wisdom : a superego function in dreams, conscience, and inspiration / by
Dan Merkur
p. cm
Includes bibliographical references and index.
ISBN 0-7914-4947-5 (hardcover : alk. paper) — ISBN 0-7914-4948-3 (pbk. : alk. paper)
1. Superego. 2. Psychoanalysis. 3. Freud, Sigmund, 1856–1936. I. Title.

BF175.5.S93 M47 2001
154.2'2—dc21
00-057329

10 9 8 7 6 5 4 3 2 1

To my good friend Keith Haartman,
whose extensive conversations contributed significantly
to this project.

If it is really the super-ego which, in humour,
speaks such kindly words of comfort to the intimidated ego,
this will teach us that we have still a great deal to learn
about the nature of the super-ego.

—Freud, "Humour" (1927b)

Contents

Acknowledgment

The first drafts of Chapters One and Three were funded by Syracuse University, Senate Committee on Research, Award No. 14, Syracuse, New York, 1987. For encouraging my interest in psychoanalysis, I am indebted to L. Bryce Boyer, M.D., Daniel M. A. Freeman, M.D., and our fellow members of the American Psychoanalytic Association's Interdisciplinary Colloquium on Psychoanalytic Questions and Methods in Anthropological Fieldwork. My thanks go also to my wife Lara Huntsman, my sons Matthew and Jeremy, and my daughter Kira, who arrived in time for the final revisions.

The author gratefully acknowledges permission to reprint materials from *The Standard Edition of the Complete Psychological Works of Sigmund Freud, Volume 5*. Edited by James Strachey. Published by Basic Books Inc. by arrangement with Hogarth Press, Ltd. and the Institute of Psycho-Analysis, London. Reprinted by permission of Basic Books, a member of Perseus Books, L.L.C., and by permission of the Random House Archive & Library, a division of the Random House Group Ltd.

Preface

Beginning with my first psychoanalytic writings, I have been explaining the evidence of religious experiences and, more generally, alternate states of consciousness in terms of positive superego functions. The prophetic words of the biblical God are manifestations of the prophet's conscience (Merkur, 1985). Visions are manifestations of conscience that have undergone symbolization in fashions consistent with the dream-work (Merkur 1985, 1989a). In trance states, conscious ego functions are repressed, and the unconscious superego assumes the executive function of the psyche (Merkur, 1984, 1988b). Mystical unions manifest ego ideals (Merkur 1989b, 1998, 1999); unitive thinking is also a versatile schema of everyday thinking (Merkur, 1999). The perceptions of miracles are projections of conscience onto fortuitous physical events (Merkur, 1999). Religious transformations are integrations of superego materials within the sense of self (Merkur, 1995–96, 1998, 1999).

In making my arguments, I have repeatedly encountered both psychoanalysts and students of religion for whom the very notion of positive superego functions is exotic, if not indeed a contradiction in terms. To deal with the communication problem, I eventually undertook an exhaustive review of the literature on the superego, out of which the present study emerged.

There turn out to be at least seven major different psychoanalytic models of the superego. Most psychoanalytic writers work with the formulations of Heinz Hartmann, Ernst Kris, and Rudolph M. Loewenstein, who were architects of the American school of psychoanalytic ego psychology. I work instead with the significantly different model of Freud.

There are two major differences between the classical and ego psychological models. Freud (1923a, p. 28) called the superego "a grade in the ego, a differentiation within the ego." He credited the psychical agency with three functions: self-observation, conscience, and ego ideals. Hartmann, Kris, and Loewenstein (1946) denied that the superego has a capacity for rational moral reflection. They expressly denied that the superego engages in either self-observation or rational thought. Hartmann and Loewenstein (1962) clarified "that 'reacting to something' should not be construed to imply 'knowing' it" and they refused "to ascribe to the superego anything that could be termed 'knowledge'" (p. 160). In effect, they denied the existence of conscience in any meaningful sense of the term.

Although Freud never did so, his model allowed Paul Schilder and Otto Kauders (1926) to speak of unconscious intelligence that the superego manifests in hypnosis. Extending the same theoretical model, this book argues that the superego routinely produces rational, intelligent reasoning, much of which is unconscious. When the unconscious reasoning is combined with the self-knowledge that the superego possesses through its access to the repressed (Freud, 1923a), unconscious wisdom results.

To make my case, I have argued the same theoretic point four different ways. Each chapter addresses a different phenomenon (dreams, judgments of conscience, creative inspirations, and metaphoric thinking), together with the history of psychoanalytic theorizing that has been devoted to it. In the first two cases I argue that phenomena generally acknowledged to be unconscious are wise; in the third, that a phenomenon known to be wise is indeed unconscious.

Together with *The Ecstatic Imagination* (Merkur, 1998) and *Mystical Moments and Unitive Thinking* (Merkur, 1999), the present volume forms a trilogy on the psychoanalysis of religious experiences. *Unconscious Wisdom* is the last of the three volumes to be published. However, the theories that it presents were developed before the other volumes were completed—indeed, before they could be completed successfully. *Unconscious Wisdom* may be read on its own as a study of dreams, conscience, and creative inspiration; but these phenomena are considered religious in most cultures the world over. A theory of religious experiences that fails to address them is necessarily incomplete—and very likely inadequate.

Introduction

In late antiquity, Jewish and Christian terms for "spirit" had two meanings. The terms denoted God's manifest power in the world. They also denoted "that aspect of man's nature which is most readily influenced by God and which is capable of taking upon itself ethical qualities of a definite nature" (Russell, 1964, p. 149). The first use of the terms pertained to the Holy Spirit; the other concerned a spirit whose indwelling within the body was believed to endow people with life (Levison, 1997). It was in the latter sense that spirit was considered the highest or noblest faculty of the human soul. Its possession was regarded as uniquely human. Nonhuman species were considered incapable of religiosity because their souls lacked spiritual faculties. Spirit was identical with intellect or reason in its natural functions, but spirit was also the faculty of the soul that received divine revelations. In some religious systems, spirit was even thought capable of divinization through its union or conjunction with the spirit of God (Rahman, 1958; Merlan, 1963; Fakhry, 1971; Blumenthal, 1977; Bland, 1982).

Among St. Paul's enduring achievements was his concept of "the law of the spirit of life" (Rom 8:2). He asserted that "the law is spiritual" (Rom 7:14) and he maintained that conscience conforms with it.

> When Gentiles, who do not possess the [Mosaic] law, do instinctively what the law requires, these, though not having the law, are a law to themselves. They show that what the law requires is written on their hearts, to which their own conscience also bears witness; and their conflicting

thoughts will accuse or perhaps excuse them on the day when, according to my gospel, God, through Jesus Christ, will judge the secret thoughts of all (Rom 2:14–16).

By "the law of the spirit of life," Paul referred explicitly to the human spirit, as distinct from the Holy Spirit. Paul's concept of the law of the spirit pertained to a natural function of the human mind that governs the judgments of conscience.

According to religious thinkers such as Philo, Paul, and Maimonides, this natural function of the mind can be educated, trained, and built up through exercise, as may any other natural endowment; and its proper development is a condition of prophecy (Heschel, 1996, pp. 104–12). The native endowment is an aptitude, as are musical, artistic, and mathematical inclinations. Its transformation into an ability or talent requires education and practice. The three thinkers recommended differing practices of spiritual direction. They agreed, however, that as long as the human spirit is inadequately cultivated, it comprehends prophecy imperfectly, contaminates grace with fantasies of the mind's invention, and so corrupts truthful revelations into false prophecies during the very process of their reception.

The mental function that late antique and medieval thinkers termed "spirit" is, I suggest, what Freud (1914) initially termed "conscience" and later (1923a) named *das Überich*, "the superego." Consider, for example, the following self-report by an American Jew of an experience that she induced through Buddhist mindfulness meditation.

Early on in my mindfulness meditation practice, I spent several weeks in intensive retreat in a monastery in Massachusetts. In the weeks just before that retreat, the entire country had followed the story of a young child with leukemia whose parents, dedicated to alternative healing, had refused to accept conventional treatment for him. The child died. Since childhood leukemia has a high cure rate with modern medicines, I was very upset about what I considered the parents' "attachment to New Age views." I was more than upset; I was mad. "How could they do this?" I thought. I was infuriated, by extension, at everything that I associated with "New Age." I was mad at newsletters and magazines and books and diet regimens and health food

stores—I was mad at anything I felt had colluded in form-
ing these parents' attachment to a view I thought had cost
the child his life. I also felt righteous in my anger, since I
was, at that time, a vegetarian, a yoga teacher, and a
meditation practitioner, and I thought I had made my choices
wisely, while other people's narrow-mindedness and rigidity were giving my choices a bad name.

I arrived at the retreat troubled by my anger. It continued for days in spite of my attempts to develop composure.
I'm fairly sure that the level of my anger was probably also
sustained by my fear about what I considered inadequate
parenting. At that time, I had young children of my own,
and the idea that parents might be so trapped by views
that they could make decisions that had such dire consequences frightened me. Every time I remembered the story,
my mind filled with anger and indignation and, finally,
resentment that these parents, strangers to me, had "destroyed my retreat by their behavior." I felt so burdened
that I prayed, "May I be *free* from this painful anger," ask-
ing that no reminder of the incident would arise in my
mind to trigger another attack of anger.

One afternoon, sitting quietly, in a moment in which
my mind was completely resting, an entirely new thought
arose: "Those parents must be in terrible pain!" And then:
"How are they going to live with themselves?" I was startled
to find that my anger had disappeared. I still believed the
refusal of medicine was a wrong choice, but I felt sad instead of mad and, at last, compassionate. "What if I made
a terrible mistake—even a well-intentioned terrible mistake—with my children? I couldn't bear it."

At the moment of my change of heart, I was so grateful
that I didn't think about how or why it had happened. I was
just glad to have been set free. It felt like a miracle. I later
discovered it is really not a miracle. It's the grace of mindfulness. Mindfulness meditation does not change life. It
changes the heart's capacity to accept it. It teaches the heart
to be more accommodating, not by beating it into submission,
but by developing wisdom (Boorstein, 1997, pp. 115–17).

The Buddhist practice of "mindfulness" (*satipatthana*) or "insight" (*vipasyana*) meditation consists of a systematic effort to detach
from the contents of one's consciousness, to observe their occurrence

without engagement in their contents, and so to become mindful of the full phenomenology of consciousness (Kornfield, 1977, 1979; Brown & Engler, 1984). In the present instance, (the practice of mindfulness led to a detachment, not from consciousness as a whole, but from self-involvement) The meditator's guilt and fear of inadequacies as a parent had been aroused by a news story, only to be displaced as intense anger at the people in the story. Where psychoanalytic insights would have intensified self-involvement by focusing on the ego and the inadequacies of its defenses against its feelings of guilt, the mindfulness meditations sought simply to let go of the ego in entirety (see Epstein, 1988).

What then emerged into consciousness was a creative solution to the problem of the underlying guilt. Through anger, the guilt had been displaced from the meditator to the parents in the news story, and it was in its displaced form that the guilt was forgiven in a moment of empathy and compassion for the parents in the news. The empathy was apparently experienced as an inspiration. It was unanticipated—"an entirely new thought arose"—and its emotional effect was startling.

Once the guilt was forgiven, the need for its displacement collapsed. The meditator was able to own the guilt and think consciously about a possible failing in her own acts as a parent. She was also consciously grateful for her release from anger—and from guilt.

Like the sense of moral responsibility, the sense of moral forgiveness is a function of judgment that is popularly ascribed to "conscience," but that psychoanalysis ascribes to the superego. Although some psychoanalytic writers treat the superego and ego ideal as separate psychical agencies, I find logical necessity in Freud's (1914; 1923; 1933) ascription of self-observation, ego ideals, and judgments of conscience to a single agency) To issue in judgments of conscience, the psyche must do three things. It must observe the ego. It must possess values, and it must apply those values as ideal standards against which it measures the ego.

When spiritual experiences do not manifest conscience, they manifest another of the superego's functions. Consider the following self-report of a unitive experience that was induced through psychedelic drug use.

Over the past eight months, and very intermittently, I've been experiencing something like a "presence"—a spiritual "fullness" or "outswelling of the spirit." . . . The zenith, thus far, of this Experience, occurred while I was on magazine-assignment in Amsterdam, this past November. I had partaken of some chemicals (but, truth be known, that is not an atypical occurrence with me, and the quantity of medicaments were in no way substantial enough to have produced the effect that I am about to put succinctly before you):

As I lay back on my cot, there was a way in which I could simultaneously relax my vision and gaze into a mirror across the room and have the light directly above the mirror refract back into my eyes . . . and

> it
> was
> as
> if
> the
> world
> fell
> away

But not—just—that. Suddenly, there was an energy component to the Experience—not just a buzzing or a humming, but a driving, all-consuming Energy. The world fell away, and suddenly I found myself in what I can only call "an energy chamber," whereupon my brain, the physical mass of my brain, felt as if it were connected to the Great Cosmic Overmind.

"I" was privy to All-Knowledge.

But that wasn't all, either. Just as suddenly, there came a spiritual infusion, which literally took my breath away. I understood then, that the Mind is one thing, and that the Spirit is another. What rushed through me and filled me and continued to fill me for some three hours, was simply Bliss.

The Energy that I felt—in that Energy Chamber—was my own. This is crucial. I was given a look at my own Life Force—and in this energy chamber, I saw several of my faces, corresponding to "me" at different ages.

That is what it was, an Energy Chamber, wherein the Energy was mine own (as if, I were being "told": "You are enough. This is it, & Now is All there is").

I remember that I was comforted to no end, knowing that the Path I was on, have been on (am on? . . . not too sure now) is/was the Right One (for me). (Prior to going to Amsterdam, doing this article, I had struggled much with "Am I living the Life I should be living?")

There came a point in this Experience, where I was prompted to ask: "Who am I?"

And the reply that came, fairly put me on my knees, weeping, for a good forty minutes. Bawling, actually. (At one point, I was sure I was going to wake up the whole hotel, and I became kind of embarrassed, and I think that is when It went away.) What came, in response to my query, was this: "You are a holy man."

And I Understood, intrinsically, what it meant to be Holy. And I was, then.

This was in November of last year. I knew not where to turn; I told very few persons about this Happening. I felt as if I were Supposed to be Doing something, but knowing not what, or in what direction, I continued on my present course (which is the marketing of a first-novel of mine, along with teaching Creative Writing at U of _____).

Lately, I have been plagued by dreams involving my (still-living) parents. There is much tension between us (my brand of prose—satire/black humor—does not sit well with them) and I feel that unless some real and meaningful resolution is found, that I will forever be in a Limbo land. . . .

Two tarot card readers and one shaman have all three said, in their report of my Condition: "You are on the brink of a transformative Awakening, which will bring to you money, will involve you in politics, and will ask of you greatly your Leadership skills; but something holds you back; you are holding yourself back," or words to that effect.

That is the long of it. Now, months away from that Experience, I do not know how to regain that sense of Rightness and Bliss. Will it come (back) to me? Is it wrong to seek it in the first place? Or, alternately, now that I have had the Experience, should I quit my bitching & live the life of a "holy man" (I assume that means, one dedicated to helping/aiding others, as opposed to a striving after fame & material success. . . . But, here again, I don't—know—that, for me. Maybe the T____ of letters, the social satirist, the black comedian, is—precisely—what is necessary, here, in the waning hours of the 20th century. . . . Maybe I—am—doing vital service toward the ushering in of an Enlightenment of some stripe . . . & if I believe that, I run the risk of being called "megalomaniacal" & "full of myself." . . . It seems like a no-win proposition. . . .)

How to proceed? This is the question that plagues me daily.

The subject reported an experience of mystical union with "the Great Cosmic Overmind." During the experience, he found himself thinking, "You are a holy man," and "You are enough. This is it, & Now is All there is." His experience of a union of energy, rightness, and bliss can be treated as a metaphoric expression of the same ideas. The spiritual insights manifested first in the form of bodily sensations and mental images, and only afterward in the form of verbal ideas. Overall, the mystical union validated the subject's sense of self through a powerful and prolonged experience of self-esteem.

Eight months after the experience, its memory continued to serve the subject as a high-water mark and an ideal for aspiration. The subject reported uncertainty whether and, if yes, how to act on the ideal. A second eight months later, the subject reported that he eventually chose to be guided by his awakening.

Truly, since then, my life has not been "the same," and I am slowly, painfully, but meaningfully, coming to an understanding of what it is to be aligned with Goodness. . . . what transpired in Amsterdam for me—which . . . [a friend] called properly "Grace"—was shattering, life-affirming, in every way a magical awakening.

In *The Ecstatic Imagination* (1998) and *Mystical Moments and Unitive Thinking* (1999), I suggested that unitive experiences articulate unconscious ego ideals. The manifest content of the experiences represents the self as ideal. An experience of mystical union is the waking equivalent of a dream symbol by whose means ego ideals are expressed. Because the unitive ideas manifest in the symbolic form of an experience, the values that are conveyed by the experience are not articulated as cognitive data that happen to be known to the self. They are not merely thought about, disinterestedly, as ideas. The values are not impersonal. The symbolism portrays the values as the self's own interests, motives, and goals. They are heartfelt, personal ideals.

The novelty of the ideals is indicated, in the above self-report, by the subject's uncertainty regarding how to act in response to them. The subject perceived the inadequacy of his existing values to direct his behavior toward the goals that he now found himself desiring. He found himself called upon to be more creative than ever previously—and specifically in the domain of what he termed "Goodness."

As an instance of the basic superego function of self-observation, consider the following account of an experience of self-transcendence.

The simplest way in which I can describe it, is as if one had been enormously absorbed in a television programme (play) to the extent that one had come to feel and believe in the reality of the people, and then, suddenly, one becomes aware for some reason that it is, after all, only a play on television. For the word 'play' use the word 'life'. Increasingly I find that at moments of complete absorption with what is happening in my life, something 'clicks' and I know it all to be a play only. Whilst I can still watch, and even partake of the 'play', something in me is aware of a far greater significance, and despite even the most harrowing and difficult happenings, there is within me, a peace which defies understanding, and knowledge that what is occurring is only the appearance. Behind this appearance, something beyond my present comprehension is slowly unfolding itself to my view. As it comes into view, I see why it had to appear in the way it did appear (Hardy, 1979, p. 64).

In this religious experience, there was a shift from the perspective of the ego into another perspective that observed the life of the ego as though it were external to the observational perspective. The ego-observing perspective contained a positive content that included both a sense of peace and cognitive manifestations of increased meaningfulness.

Perhaps because most studies of religious experiences do not closely review individual self-reports, but instead either speculate philosophically or quantify statistically, a basic fact has repeatedly escaped attention. Not only do the self-reports claim a cognitive or intellectual depth to their experiences, but the logical or rational character of the religious inspirations is undeniable. At least some religious experiences are creative inspirations of values and ideals that articulate the highest aspirations of the individuals involved. These experiences are neither irrational, as Freud and Jung both claimed, nor nonrational, as Rudolf Otto (1951) suggested. The religious experiences are eminently reasonable, rational, realistic, thoughtful, and profound.

Philo, Paul, and Maimonides believed that the cultivation of the human spirit was both possible and religiously desirable. In the practice of mysticism, no differently than in psychotherapy, "one's model . . . has an organizing effect, it selects our responses and interpretations; our theoretical preconceptions determine how we conduct an analysis" (Modell, 1987, p. 233; cf. Meissner, 1982, p. 27). What is at issue in this book is a point of theory. What is at stake are its consequences for both spirituality and psychotherapy.

Chapter 1

THE COHERENCE OF THE DREAM-WORK

Psychoanalytic theorizing begins with the fact that conscious thought is coherent or, at least, ordinarily capable of coherence, whereas the manifest content of dreams is often partly or wholly incoherent. Sigmund Freud's (1900) *Interpretation of Dreams* makes the methodological claim that incoherent images and ideas can be rendered coherent through their interpretation as symbols whose meanings are unconscious. As Fliess (1973) remarked, "If a sequence of thought contains gaps that can be closed only by reading certain elements in it symbolically, then they are symbols" (p. 17). To explain why the psychoanalytic method of dream interpretation appears to work, Freud hypothesized that the unconscious mind produces dreams by translating the contents of conscious and rational ("secondary process") ideas into images, of which some are manifestly incoherent or irrational ("primary process").

In 1900, when Freud presented what came to be called the "topographic hypothesis" of the psyche, he allocated all rational thought to the system *Perception-Consciousness (Pcpt.-Cs.)* and only irrational symbol-formation to the system *Unconscious (Ucs.)*. Carl G. Jung's position was closely derivative. Although Jung (1938, p. 45) recognized that "the unconscious mind is capable at times of assuming an intelligence and purposiveness which are superior to

1

actual conscious insight," the observation, which was presumably clinical, was never formally expressed in theory. In Jung's theory system, archetypes are unconscious instinctual forms that manifest conscious images whenever there is a quantitative imbalance in the distribution of psychic energy between consciousness and the unconscious. The intelligence and compensatory function of archetypal manifestations is an automatic consequence of the design of the objective psyche. It is analogous to a thermostat turning an air conditioner on and off. The unconscious does not reason. It remains limited to irrational symbol formation.

The exclusive irrationality of unconscious thinking, which both Freudians and Jungians have since taken for granted, may be contrasted, for example, with the views of William James (1902) and Evelyn Underhill (1910). In their classic contributions to the psychology of religion, James and Underhill argued that the emotional crises that surround conversion and the *via mystica*, respectively, are products of conscious resistance to unconscious religious materials. James and Underhill postulated a highly intelligent, rational unconsciousness (*inter alia*, as the recipient of divine grace).

Freud implied the validity of postulating unconscious rationality when he expanded his model of the psyche in 1923. In what came to be termed the "structural hypothesis," Freud introduced the terms "id" to describe the primary, irrational process of the unconscious and "ego" for the secondary, rational process of consciousness. He also subdivided secondary process thought into the systems ego and superego, and he recognized that the superego has an unconscious extension.

Freud nowhere explicitly acknowledged that the superego's unconscious performance of secondary process thought constitutes an unconscious, rational intelligence. However, Paul Schilder and Otto Kauders (1926) drew psychoanalytic attention to "sleep vigils" that remain awake when the rest of the mind sleeps. They cited "the mother who can be aroused only by the crying of her own child; the miller who awakens when his mill stops" (p. 67). These vigils are instances of intelligent unconscious responses to sense perceptions. Other feats of the sleep vigil are still more instructive. Many people can awaken from sleep at a designated time (p. 68)— for example, a minute before an alarm clock. To explain the extraordinary achievements of the sleep vigil, Schilder and Kauders suggested that "it must attend to minor tasks only which it then

carried out with greater precision" (p. 68) than the wakii
They attributed the sleep vigil to the ego ideal (p. 76), which they
considered "an integral part of the superego" (p. 75, n. 1), and they
extrapolated from the sleep vigil to the hypnotic state.

Parsimony, rather than logical necessity, was responsible for
the assignment to the superego of the unconscious intelligence that
manifests in both the sleep vigil and hypnosis. It may not be assigned to the ego because the ego is unconscious of it; and it may
not be assigned to the id because the primary process is irrational.
If a fourth psychic agency is not to be postulated, the unconscious
intelligence must be assigned to the superego.

In this connection, I would emphasize Freud's (1923a) observation that the superego is better informed than the ego because it
has access, as the ego does not, to the contents of the repressed.
Schilder and Kauders suggested that because the superego can
devote more time to single problems than the ego can afford to do,
it can arrive at more intelligent solutions. The combination of more
extensive self-knowledge and greater concentrated intelligence in
the handling of limited topics constitutes what I shall call unconscious wisdom.

Freud never integrated his theory of the superego with his
work on dreams. Reissues of *The Interpretation of Dreams* included
a footnote that identified the dream censorship as the superego;
and Freud suggested that some dreams, which he called "dreams
from above," manifested superego materials. Otherwise, he basi-
cally let his original formulations stand. The oversight has yet to
be corrected.

Anna Freud remarked that for many decades she and many
other psychoanalysts used both the topographic and the structural
models of the mind in alternation, depending on whether, for example, they were momentarily concerned with dreams or defense
mechanisms. "I definitely belong to the people who feel free to fall
back on the topographical aspects whenever convenient, and to
leave them aside and to speak purely structurally when that is
convenient" (Sandler with Freud, 1985, p. 31). In similar fashions,
Lewin (1952), Arlow and Brenner (1964), and Kohut (1984) stated
that most of their contemporaries reverted to the topographic hypothesis whenever they conceptualized dreams. Under the circumstances, the superego's unconscious contributions to dreams went
unexplored.

As a person who habitually relies on the unconscious incubation of ideas—both everyday problems that I "sleep on" overnight, and major efforts of creativity—I do not doubt the occurrence in dreams of unconscious wisdom. I know from frequent experience that my unconscious is both smarter and wiser than my waking consciousness, but always in addressing specific limited topics. Because most psychoanalysts do not recognize the rationality of the unconscious, I presume that they interpret dreams differently than I do.

It happens that Freud's *Interpretation of Dreams* (1900) was the first work by Freud that I read, and I have applied its model to dreams ever since. Dream interpretation as Freud originally outlined it differed from the procedure that he discussed in his later publications. *The Interpretation of Dreams* does not integrate the sexual theories that Freud first published in 1905. We know from Freud's letters to Wilhelm Fliess that he had already developed the sexual theories in 1899. As a consequence, even as the epoch-making dream book went to press, its author was abandoning the clinical technique that he recommended in it.

The innovation in technique that is reflected in Freud's later writings on dreams did not arise from a change in dream theory. The innovation was designed to save time in therapy. Once Freud arrived at his sexual theories, he developed an abbreviated method of dream interpretation that focused on unconscious infantile sexuality, and he habitually neglected many other aspects of dreams that he had discussed in detail in 1900. He never renounced his initial findings—he simply did not work with them clinically. Neither have psychoanalysts since.

A notable exception to this generalization is Robert J. Langs (1988; 1992; 1994b; 1999), who has discussed "unconscious wisdom processing" in several recent works. Langs is a highly original and controversial theorist who has invented his own model of the psyche (1986; 1987a; 1987b) as well as a clinical technique that he terms "communicative psychoanalysis." Lang's first book on dream interpretation (1988) is less idiosyncratic than his later presentations and has much to recommend it.

Unlike Langs, I see neither need nor advantage to depart from the tripartite model of the mind. The experiential reality of the unconscious wisdom of dreams can be formulated through superego theory in a fashion consistent with Schilder and Kauders's notion of the sleep vigil. Let us review dream theory in its light.

Wish-Fulfillment Theory

The experience of interpreting hundreds of dreams led Freud (1900) to his general thesis that "the meaning of *every* dream is the fulfilment of a wish" (p. 134). Freud's formulation combined two claims.

1. Dreams are meaningful, motivated, and purposeful; they are not random, meaningless, and incoherent gibberish.

2. Unlike motivations, intentions, and desires, dreams involve more than wishing; they portray the fulfilling of wishes.

The fundamental premise of Freud's theory, that dreams are purposive, is not altered by changing fashions that refer to wishes by such terms as instincts, drives, desires, motives, and interests. The alternative to wish-fulfillment theory is not its qualification through a minor nuance, but the categorical claim that dreams are random, unmotivated, and nonpurposive gibberish. Because Freud's theory was based on the evidence not of dreams but of their interpretations during conscious states, his case was inconclusive. On Freud's showing, it was conceivable that the motivation disclosed through dream interpretation was read into dreams by their interpreters. The logical force of my argument differs. I am arguing that dream interpretations often exhibit wisdom greater than the conscious abilities of their interpreters. The interpretations have the power to surprise both dreamers and interpreters with their wisdom. Since the wisdom cannot reasonably be treated as an invention of consciousness subsequent to the dreams, neither can the wishes to which the wisdom responds.

As to the second part of his thesis, Freud (1940) eventually moderated it by stating that "a dream is invariably an *attempt*" to fulfill a wish. "The attempt may succeed more or less completely; it may also fail" (p. 171). A dream may portray an unsuccessful attempt to fulfill the wish; it never fails to portray an attempt. On the other hand, Freud's thesis that dreams are constructed in the form of wish-fulfillments does not imply that fulfilling wishes is the raison d'être of dreams (Dement, 1964, p. 151).

Freud (1908a) presented the basic ideas of wish-fulfillment theory most succinctly in the course of a discussion of daydreaming.

> Mental work is linked to some current impression, some pro-voking occasion in the present which has been able to arouse one of the subject's major wishes. From there it harks back to a memory of an earlier experience (usually an infantile one) in which this wish was fulfilled; and it now creates a situation relating to the future which represents a fulfilment of the wish. What it thus creates is a day-dream or phantasy, which carries about it traces of its origin from the occasion which provoked it and from the memory (p. 148).

A wish that is not presently being satisfied is associated with the memory of a wish that was satisfied. When the two wishes are unconsciously equated, the satisfaction of the past wish becomes the fantasied satisfaction of the present wish.

A wish-fulfillment always compounds two separate wishes. It is the past wish whose habitual use may cause it to function, in Jean Piaget's terminology, as a cognitive "schema." Unfortunately, Freud often lapsed rhetorically into the singular, for example, in his state-ment that the unsatisfying present wish "harks back to a memory . . . in which this wish was fulfilled" (Freud, 1908a, p. 148). In another phrasing, Freud (1900) clearly distinguished the past and present wishes, respectively, as the "wish" and the "source" of the dream. "The source of a dream," he wrote, is always "one or more recent and significant experiences" (p. 180). In the passage adduced above, Freud referred discretely to the present wish as the "motive force" of the daydream.

Freud (1900) regarded symbol-formation as the whole of the unconscious process of dreaming. "Dreams are nothing other than a particular *form* of thinking, made possible by the conditions of the state of sleep. It is the *dream-work* which creates that form, and it alone is the essence of dreaming" (pp. 506–7 n. 2). Freud imagined that the condensation of the present and unsatisfied wish with the memory of a wish that was satisfied in the past, automati-cally and mechanically portrays the present wish as fulfilled.

The coherent meaning that a dream's psychoanalytic interpretation purportedly reconstructs is termed the "dream-thought" or "latent content" of the dream. Freud assumed, again *ex hypothesi*, that the process of dreaming makes use of latent dream-thoughts that have already been formed preconsciously during wakefulness. Dreaming is limited to their secondary conversion into symbolic forms. Freud (1900) treated the dream-thoughts and their symbolization (the "dream-work") as mutually exclusive processes. "Everything that appears in dreams as the ostensible activity of the function of judgement is to be regarded not as an intellectual achievement of the dream-work but as belonging to the material of the dream-thoughts and as having been lifted from them into the manifest content of the dream as a ready-made structure" (p. 445).

Freud similarly attributed the occasional intelligence of the dream to preconscious thought. He claimed that the ideas are developed during wakefulness when preconscious secondary process thought elaborates the unsatisfied wishes of the day. "The fact that dreams concern themselves with attempts at solving the problems by which our mental life is faced is no more strange than that our conscious waking life should do so; beyond this it merely tells us that that activity can also be carried on in the preconscious—and this we already know" (pp. 506–7 n. 2).

Symbolization

Under the term "dream-work" Freud (1900) initially discussed four phenomena by which latent dream-thoughts are converted into the manifest dream-contents: condensation, displacement, considerations of representability, and secondary revision. Two later formulations restricted the dream-work to the first three phenomena (Freud, 1913; 1923d). With secondary revision excluded from discussion, dream-work became synonymous with "symbolization": the conversion of the latent dream thoughts into manifest dream imagery.

Considerations of Representability

Freud (1900) regarded the manifest dream-content as a "transcript . . . as it were in a pictographic script" (p. 277). Considerations of representability refer to the limited ability of the "pictographic script" of perceptual fantasies to express abstract ideas. The considerations are imposed during "the transformation of the dream-thoughts into the dream-contents" (pp. 343–44). Considerations of representability may be counted as the first aspect of symbolization. Both adults and children report some dreams that involve no further types of symbolization. "These well-organized dreams may portray 'cure,' or perhaps sudden good fortune, like winning a lottery, or sexual success ... these dreams make sense and tell coherent stories; at times it is difficult to be sure whether we are listening to an account of a dream or to that of an actual event" (Stein, 1989, p. 68).

Laboratory dream research has augmented but has not significantly altered these aspects of the clinical picture. Although coherent dreams are rarely reported clinically, they appear experimentally to form a majority of dream experience.

> About 90 percent of REM dreams are judged to be about as credible as descriptions of waking reality, equally undramatic and lacking in bizarreness. ... REM dream reports are generally clear, coherent, believable accounts of realistic situations in which the dreamer and other persons are involved in quite mundane activities and preoccupations. ... Reports were considered almost entirely representational and realistic in visual form, generally involving a familiar or commonplace setting, almost always including the self, usually in interaction with other persons. The most typical interaction described is verbal in nature ... REM dreams seem to be almost as much auditory as visual experiences (Snyder, 1967, in Trosman, 1969, pp. 58–59).

Coherent dreams have also been reported following arousal from NREM sleep (Whitman, Kramer, Ornstein, & Baldridge, 1967, p. 293; Cartwright, 1969, pp. 362–63). "The mental activity from nonREM awakenings is thoughtlike and can be distinguished from the perceptual, storylike, and sometimes bizarre content that occurs during REM sleep" (Greenberg, Katz, Schwartz, & Pearlman, 1992).

The conversion of latent fantasy ideation into concrete perceptual imagery may similarly be the total extent of symbol-formation both in daydreams and hypnagogic states. The "transcription of thoughts into pictures in the hypnagogic state occurs in relative isolation from other dream-forming factors" (Silberer, 1909, p. 197).

To account for the unconscious translation of verbally expressed thoughts into perceptual forms, Freud suggested that dreams accommodate an inherent limitation of the *Ucs. Ex hypothesi* unconscious thought differs from conscious thought not only in its access to consciousness, but also in its mental elements. The dream-work's reduction of verbal ideas to sense images, emotions, and motor ideas is comprehensible if the *Ucs.* cannot understand higher order ideation.

Freud (1900) assumed that all dream-thoughts commence in the form of abstract (verbally expressed) ideas and subsequently undergo reversion to the concrete (perceptual) images from which they were abstracted (pp. 118, 277). Kohut and other analysts have recognized, however, that the generalization admits exceptions (Edelheit, 1968). No differently than conscious thinking, dreaming may utilize what psychoanalysts call "concrete ideas": "mental images"; spatial, musical, and other sensory ideas; pattern perceptions; and so forth. In such cases, the secondary process ideas are already in perceptual forms, and a further transcription is unnecessary.

Condensation

Freud found marked discrepancies in the extent and expressiveness of dreams and their interpretations. "Dreams are brief, meagre and laconic in comparison with the range and wealth of the dream-thoughts" (Freud, 1900, p. 279). He postulated that a single symbol may express a plurality of latent ideas as a consequence of an unconscious process that he termed condensation. The motifs are then said to be overdetermined. Condensation is not a response to censorship (Freud, 1916–17). Like considerations of representability, condensation is an accommodation of the primary process. Because the primary process works with only a small range of emotions, sensations, and motor ideas, secondary process ideas must be rendered concrete and reduced to the limited vocabulary of instinctual desire before an unsatisfied wish can gain unconscious associations and be fantasied as fulfilled. Condensation accomplishes the reduction.

Emotion plays a distinctive role in condensation. Freud (1900) noted that "in dreams the ideational content is not accompanied by the affective consequences that we should regard as inevitable in waking thought" (p. 461). He suggested "that the affect felt in the dream belongs to its latent and not to its manifest content, and that the dream's *affective* content has remained untouched by the distortion which has overtaken its *ideational* content" (pp. 248–49). He also suggested that the dream-work's preservation of affect functioned as a criterion or organizing principle for the association of dream materials. "During the dream-work, sources of affect which are capable of producing the same affect come together in generating it" (p. 480).

Displacement

Again on the basis of his practice of dream interpretation, Freud (1900) hypothesized that "the elements which stand out as the principal components of the manifest content of the dream are far from playing the same part in the dream-thoughts . . . what is clearly the essence of the dream-thoughts need not be represented in the dream at all" (p. 305). To account for these discrepancies, Freud postulated the activity of an unconscious process that he termed "displacement" (p. 306).

It thus seems plausible to suppose that in the dream-work a psychical force is operating which on the one hand strips the elements which have a high psychical value of their intensity, and on the other hand, *by means of overdetermination*, creates from elements of low psychical value new values, which afterwards find their way into the dream-content. If that is so, *a transference and displacement of psychical intensities* occurs in the process of dream-formation, and it is as a result of these that the difference between the text of the dream-content and that of the dream-thoughts comes about (pp. 307–8; Freud's italics).

Because displacement distorts the manifest content of a dream, Freud speculated that displacement is a response to a process of censorship that prevents the latent content from manifesting consciously in undisguised form (p. 308). "The censorship exercises its office and brings about the distortion of dreams . . . in order to prevent the generation of anxiety or other forms of distressing affect" (p. 267).

The Metaphor of Regression

Freud was never able to locate the process of symbolization within his heuristic model of the mind as a "psychic apparatus." Freud's writings (1901a, p. 676; 1910a, p. 36; 1915b, pp. 153–54; 1915c, p. 190; 1916–17, p. 212) are decisive in their arrival at a quandary. Freud maintained that ideas are unconsciously transformed into symbols in order to evade a censorship that prevents their conscious manifestation. Because he consistently credited the censorship to the secondary process, the evasion of censorship by recourse to symbolization could not logically be assigned to the same secondary process. However, Freud could not logically ascribe the translation of verbal ideas into perceptual form to the primary process either. The primary process does not perform verbal ideation. Neither has it a capacity to understand verbal ideation. What it cannot understand, it cannot translate into its own considerably limited, concrete mental elements. Because fantasy is a compromise formation that reduces secondary process ideas to the forms of primary process materials, Freud (1910a, p. 36) inferred that fantasy is produced "in the unconscious, or rather, to put it more accurately, between two separate psychical systems like the conscious and unconscious."

Freud arrived at his concept of symbolization as a compromise formation through a process of elimination. Symbolization could not be a secondary process because it is censored by the secondary process; yet symbolization could not be a primary process because symbolization makes ideational uses of perceptual imagery in treating them as symbols. For the same reasons, symbolization cannot be a collaboration of the primary and secondary processes. It is an exception to both, occurring in neither, but somehow located in the interstices between the two.

Freud (1900) provided a detailed model of the conversion of latent ideas into concrete perceptual images. "We call it 'regression' when in a dream an idea is turned back into the sensory image from which it was originally derived. . . . *In regression the fabric of the dream-thoughts is resolved into its raw material"* (p. 543). Because Freud (1900, p. 548; 1916–17, pp. 342–43; 1917a, pp. 227–28) later distinguished varieties of regression, the resolution of verbal ideation into perceptual images came technically to be termed *topographic regression*. Topographic regression reverses the preconscious process of verbal recognition. It is a fitting of perceptual images to verbal ideas, rather than vice versa. In the topographic hypothesis, Freud (1900) considered topographic regression responsible also for *temporal regression*, which is a return to mentation consistent with an earlier developmental stage. Every wish-fulfillment was therefore necessarily infantile. Freud's (1923a) structural model of the mind instead recognized that the two types of regression are independent variables. Either may occur in the absence of the other.

Freud's account of symbolization through topographic regression is not a coherent theory, but only a metaphor that covers a gap in close theoretic reasoning. The metaphor extends Freud's analogy of the psychical apparatus to a reflex arc. In a mechanical reflex arc, such as a toy that is powered by tightening a spring that drives the toy as it unwinds, every increase in energy potential is a progression toward its tightened position, and every decrease a regression. Although the metaphor of a reflex arc served Freud well as long as he used it in a loose, heuristic manner that made it equivalent to what we today term "biofeedback," pressing the metaphor unduly led Freud into fallacy. The model of a reflex arc is at best a metaphor for psychological purposes. It does not accurately reflect the real circumstance of the psyche, among other reasons, because neurons only fire in one direction. It is not possible that a reversion from the secondary to the primary process can be accomplished by the same neurons that construct secondary process ideas on the basis of primary process sensations. At minimum, a physiological model of the mind would require the postulation of a parallel set of neurons that point in the opposing direction.

Although many scientific discoveries are initially apprehended in the form of metaphors, the replacement of metaphor with closely reasoned theory is a condition of subsequent scientific progress (Langer, 1957, pp. 102, 201–2; Grossman, 1992, p. 55). Uncritical perpetuation of the metaphor of topographic regression is an impediment to psychoanalytic theory. Freud's notion (1910a, p. 36) that fantasy is produced, as it were, in the interstices "between two separate psychical systems like the conscious and unconscious" extended the metaphor of topographic regression to the point of absurdity.

On one early occasion Freud (1901b, p. 147) speculated that symbolization might be the product of a "lower psychical agency," and the suggestion remains a viable theoretical option. A retroversion from secondary to primary process thought cannot be accomplished as a regression. There can be no simple mechanical retroversion. Any such concept is mere metaphor. What occurs is a complex and intelligent process of *translation* that reduces secondary process ideas to forms that are capable of communicating with the primary process (Brenner, 1973, p. 172). If the work of translation is to succeed—that is, if a present frustration is to be associated with an unconscious instinctual desire, so that a wish-fulfillment may be elaborated—the presently unsatisfied wish must be translated into a form that is consistent with the primary process. It is untenable that the work of translation is accomplished by the same psychical agency whose limitations necessitate its performance. The translating process is bilingual; the primary process is not. If the primary process were bilingual, a translation process would not be necessary. The semantic or lexical limitations of the primary process both necessitate the process of translation and impose constraints on it.

Consider, for example, the analogy of a computer program that is upgraded at a later time. The upgrade can process any ideas that the original program can produce, but there is much that the upgrade can produce that the original program cannot compute. A translation program that converts upgrade formats into the original format is necessary before the "primary process" can work with "secondary process" ideas. The translation is limited by considerations of primary process representability, but the translation program constitutes a third piece of software in its own right.

Secondary Revision

Freud attributed the partial coherence of manifest dreams to a process that he termed "secondary revision" and explained in different ways over the years (Breznitz, 1971; Stein, 1989). He always held to his initial description of the manifest phenomenon: "Those parts of a dream on which the secondary revision has been able to produce some effect are clear, while those parts on which its efforts have failed are confused" (Freud, 1900, p. 500). Freud maintained that secondary revision differs in its purpose from symbolization. "This function . . . fills up the gaps in the dream-structure with shreds and patches" (p. 490).

Freud initially attributed secondary revision to the dream-censorship. "There can be no doubt that the censoring agency, whose influence we have so far only recognized in limitations and omissions in the dream-content, is also responsible for interpolations and additions in it" (p. 489). "The secondary (and often ill-conceived) revision of the dream by the agency which carries out normal thinking . . . is itself no more than a part of the revision to which the dream-thoughts are regularly subjected as a result of the dream-censorship" (p. 514). The censorship "has the power to create new contributions to dreams," "exerts its influence principally by its preferences and selections from psychic material in the dream-thoughts that has already been formed" and "seeks to mould the material offered to it into something like a day-dream" (pp. 491–92).

Only a few pages after Freud attributed secondary revision to the censorship, he radically qualified these formulations and transformed the term "secondary revision" into a misnomer. On the strength of a persuasive demonstration that secondary revision may save labor by utilizing preexisting daydreams that happen to be available in memory, Freud denied that revisions of *unconscious* dream symbolism ever occur (pp. 495–98). Revisions occur, but Freud maintained that they are invariably *preconscious*.

Freud's lifelong habit of publishing the unrevised first drafts of his ideas was presumably responsible for allowing this self-contradiction to see print. In Freud's second formulation, secondary revision occurs before symbolization, and not vice versa. The revision is not a process of rationalization that links incoherent dream-symbols in a specious manner (cf. Nunberg, [1932] 1955, p. 151). The preconscious thinking contributes to the coherence of the manifest dream only indirectly. It contributes directly to the coherence of the latent dream-thoughts. Astoundingly, this formulation rendered Freud's initial theory meaningless! Only a secondary revision that is truly secondary, because it occurs *after* symbol-formation, could be said to rationalize the manifest dream without participating in its latent content. Secondary revision, as Freud had defined it only a few pages earlier, did not exist.

In the middle years of his psychoanalytic career, Freud entirely abandoned the idea of secondary revision. In his first account of dream-work, Freud (1900) had defined fantasy as co-extensive with secondary revision and daydreams. When several years later he considered daydreams closely, Freud (1908a) expanded his definition of fantasy to include latent dream-thoughts as a whole.

Our dreams at night are nothing else than phantasies. . . . If the meaning of our dreams usually remains obscure to us in spite of this pointer, it is because of the circumstance that at night there also arise in us wishes of which we are ashamed; these we must conceal from ourselves, and they have consequently been repressed, pushed into the unconscious. Repressed wishes of this sort and their derivatives are only allowed to come to expression in a very distorted form (pp. 148–49).

Here Freud recognized fantasy as a genus of which daydreams, latent dream-thoughts, and hysterical dream-states (Freud, 1908b) are species. Daydreams may depend less on symbolization and more on rational thinking than dreams do, but the process of fantasying is the same in both cases. The variable factor is the extent to which waking and sleeping fantasies make use of displacements.

Freud's new definition of fantasy corrected the misnomer "secondary revision" by rendering the very concept superfluous. If dreams are fantasies, and secondary revisions are fantasy's contributions to the dream-work, secondary revisions are synonymous with dreams themselves. Two later publications were consistent with this new definition. Freud (1913; 1923d) twice dispensed with secondary revision and restricted the dream-work to condensation, displacement, and considerations of representability.

However, in his final formulations of dream theory, Freud (1933) amended his position in yet another regard. He reintroduced the concept of secondary revision, but he now claimed that it is introduced within a dream only "after the dream has been presented before consciousness as an object of perception" (p. 21). With this argument, Freud was at last able to sustain his view of secondary revision as a superficial rationalization of the manifest dream-content.

> The outcome of the dream-work is a compromise. The ego-organization is not yet paralyzed, and its influence is to be seen in the distortion imposed on the unconscious material and in what are often very ineffective attempts at giving the total result a form not too unacceptable to the ego (*secondary revision*) (Freud, 1940, p. 167).

Freud's three accounts of the manifest coherence of dreams had in common a categorical denial that rational thought contributes to the unconscious dream-work. Either secondary revision is a misnomer for preconscious elaborations of unsatisfied wishes prior to sleep; or secondary revision does not occur at all; or secondary revision takes place in consciousness in response to the manifestation of dreams. In all cases, there is no such thing as unconscious wisdom.

Freud's Argument from Theory

Freud (1900) always categorically denied that the unconscious processes of the dream-work can give origin to coherent thought. However, he offered no evidence in support of his assertion. His argument on this point proceeded from theory, not from fact. In discussing the manifest coherence of some dreams, or parts of dreams, he reasoned:

> Are we to suppose that what happens is that in the first instance the dream-constructing factors—the tendency towards condensation, the necessity for evading censorship, and considerations of representability by the psychical means open to dreams—put together a provisional dream-content out of the material provided, and that this content is subsequently recast so as to conform so far as possible to the demands of a second [and rational] agency? This is scarcely probable. We must assume rather that from the very first the demands of this second factor constitute one of the conditions which the dream must satisfy (p. 499).

The cogency of Freud's argument depended on his assumption that the psychic apparatus is limited to two psychic agencies. Only *Pcpt.-Cs.* was rational. It alone could be responsible for the coherence in dreams. However, because *Pcpt.-Cs.* (a) is so relaxed that dreams have the hallucinatory quality of seeming real and (b) imposes the repression that dream-thoughts evade through symbolization, *Pcpt.-Cs.* cannot reasonably be thought to recast provisional fantasy contents.

The structural hypothesis of the id, ego, and superego (Freud, 1923a) rendered these arguments unnecessary. Unlike the topographic model of *Pcpt.-Cs.* and *Ucs.* (Freud, 1900), the structural hypothesis did not limit coherent thought to consciousness. The recasting of provisional fantasy contents could still not be assigned to the repressing agency, which was now named the ego (Freud, 1923a; 1926). However, Freud acknowledged that much superego activity was unconscious, and its involvement in dream formation was a viable theoretic option.

By the superego, Freud (1923a, pp. 35–37) described a psychic agency that he had earlier termed "conscience" (1914, pp. 95–98) and the "ego ideal" (1921, p. 110). Under all its names, Freud (1933) ascribed three functions to the agency:

> Conscience is one of its functions and . . . self-observation, which is an essential preliminary to the judging activity of conscience, is another of them. . . . It is also the vehicle of the ego ideal by which the ego measures itself, which it emulates, and whose demand for ever greater perfection it strives to fulfill (pp. 60, 65).

Freud had been aware of the influence of conscience on dreams from 1900 onward. Drawing on his experience with the psychotherapy of neurosis, Freud (1900) asserted that "whenever one psychical element [in the manifest dream] is linked with another by an objectionable or superficial association, there is also a legitimate and deeper link between them" (p. 530). Freud attributed the disappearance of the latent link to a process of censorship. He suggested that the censorship's purpose is to avoid distress, and that latent dream-thoughts undergo displacement in order to accommodate it. "The censorship exercises its office and brings about the distortion of dreams . . . in order to prevent the generation of

anxiety or other forms of distressing affect" (p. 267). Freud speculated that censorship is imposed by an agency that has the
"privilege . . . of permitting thoughts to enter consciousness" (p. 144).
On this theory, the extent to which a wish-fulfillment undergoes
displacement varies in direct relation with the censorship that the
symbols seek to evade. Dreams occur during sleep rather than
wakefulness because "the state of sleep . . . reduces the power of
the endopsychic censorship" (p. 526). During wakefulness, the censorship is more thorough. Not even highly distorted materials are
allowed to manifest consciously.

Freud (1900, pp. 615, 617–18; 1915c, pp. 173, 191, 193–94) twice
raised the possibility that dreams encounter two censorships: (1)
repression between the unconscious repressed and preconscious
thought, and (2) another stimulus barrier between preconscious and
conscious thought. He never expressed the idea of two censorships
in terms of psychical agencies. However, he seems to have entertained the concept while avoiding the phraseology. A censorship
that responds to psychic paralysis and helplessness by instituting
repression operates differently than a censorship that expresses
approval and disapproval, but enforces nothing. The tripartite model
of the mind firmly separated the two functions by attributing the
task of repressing to the ego, but moral censure to the superego.

In keeping with the attribution of dream-censorship to repression in the topographic hypothesis, Freud's (1923a) initial presentation of the structural hypothesis stated that the ego "exercises
the censorship on dreams" (p. 17). The superego can motivate the
ego's work of repression (Freud, 1933, p. 98), but it cannot enforce
it. However, later in the same year and for the rest of his life,
Freud (1923b) reversed himself and attributed the censorship of
dreams to the superego. "To the mental force in human beings
which . . . distorts the dream's primitive instinctual impulses in
favour of conventional or of higher moral standards, I gave the
name of 'dream-censorship'" (p. 262; cf. 1914, p. 97; 1916–17, p.
429; 1933, pp. 27–28). With the notable exception of repression,
almost everything that Freud had attributed to the dream-censorship since 1900 had pertained to what he was now calling the
superego, rather than to the ego.

Freud (1900) had always recognized that the dream-censorship
is able to contribute original materials to the manifest dream. "The

psychical agency which otherwise operates only as a censorship plays a *habitual* part in the construction of dreams. . . . There can be no doubt that the censoring agency, whose influence we have . . . recognized in limitations and omissions in the dream-content, is also responsible for interpolations and additions in it" (p. 489). In his *Introductory Lectures on Psycho-Analysis*, Freud (1916–17) emphasized that "the dream-censorship itself is the originator, or one of the originators, of the dream-distortion" (p. 140; cf. pp. 168, 233); and he expressly linked the motivation of the distortions to conscience (p. 429).

When Freud introduced the structural model of the mind and attributed these limited influences on dreams to the superego, he was presenting exceptions to his categorical rejection of the possibility that some latent dream-thoughts have unconscious origin. He was himself advancing a theory of unconscious wisdom. Unlike the ego, which is quiescent during sleep, conscience is active in dreams as the dream-censorship and contributes original symbols to the manifest dream-content. However, Freud never systematically phrased dream theory in structural terms, and so never developed the logical corollaries of his own arguments.

Had Freud ever done so, the superego's active involvement in the dream-work would have been a necessary postulate. When a person sleeps, the conscious functions of the psyche relax. Both less important and voluntarily inhibited psychic materials, neither of which are conscious during wakefulness, have the opportunity during sleep to attract such attention as remains active (cf. Freud, 1900, pp. 590–91; Meissner, 1968, pp. 75–77). According to the structural model of the psyche, the principal divisions of unconscious thought are: the instincts, the repressed, the repressing, and the unconscious reach of the superego. It is only to be expected, then, that the superego would be among the chief contributors to dreams.

Freud's failure to recognize the extent of the superego's contribution to the dream-work may be attributed to oversight. His oversight was both theoretic and clinical, and led him systematically to discount clinical evidence to the contrary. To account for superego contributions to dreams, Freud (1923c) postulated a separate type of dream that he called "dreams from above."

It is possible to distinguish between dreams *from above* and dreams *from below*, provided the distinction is not made too sharply. Dreams from below are those which are provoked by the strength of an unconscious (repressed) wish which has found a means of being represented in some of the day's residues. They may be regarded as inroads of the repressed into waking life. Dreams from above correspond to thoughts or intentions of the day before which have contrived during the night to obtain reinforcement from repressed material that is debarred from the ego. When this is so, analysis as a rule disregards this unconscious ally and succeeds in inserting the latent dream-thoughts into the texture of waking thought (p. 111).

Freud's concept of dreams "from above" reflected the necessity to account for dreams whose wisdom is so blatant that it cannot be denied. In such cases, Freud acknowledged the rationality but denied its unconscious origin by postulating its derivation "from above."

Freud's division of dreams into superego dreams "from above" and id dreams "from below" was clinically and theoretically incorrect. Every dream is both a dream from above and a dream from below (cf. Palombo, 1978). It is a condensation of a present wish with a past one. The latent dream-thoughts have preconscious origin in the day residue, while the choice of dream symbolism has unconscious origin and a second order of latent meaning. The relative importance or prominence of each wish contributes distinctive character, so that some dreams are mostly from above and others mostly from below; but all dreams invariably include both components.

What alone truly differs in dreams from above and below is the manner of the analyst's method of dream interpretation: from above, in terms of the unsatisfied wish that is contained in the day residue (see Langs, 1988; 1991; 1994b; 1999); or from below, in terms of the unconscious wish that shapes its symbolism. In my own view, the traditional psychoanalytic prioritizing of interpretations "from below" systematically neglects the unconscious wisdom of dreams. Psychoanalysts systematically skew dream interpretation through one-sided emphases of the psychosexual and psycho-aggressive elements in dreams, and through an equally categorical neglect of their rational features.

The error's motive is transparent. What was at stake in Freud's claim that dreaming consisted exclusively of symbolization, to the exclusion of rational thinking, was his epoch-making demonstration of the importance of unconscious thought. In 1900, Freud needed to establish the very existence of the system *Ucs.* His need to argue his thesis, without dissipating its force through digressions onto other issues, encouraged him to limit his claims about the dream-work to symbol-formation to the exclusion of "the function of judgment." The occurrence of dreaming during the unconsciousness of sleep could be cited in support of the postulation of the system *Ucs.* only in reference to those aspects of dreaming that differ categorically from waking thoughts. Freud wrote:

The dream-work is not simply more careless, more irrational, more forgetful and more incomplete than waking thought; it is completely different from it qualitatively and for that reason not immediately comparable with it. It does not think, calculate or judge in any way at all; it restricts itself to giving things a new form (p. 507).

Because the dream-thoughts could be attributed to the system *Pcpt.-Cs.*, Freud could not prove his case by referring to them. Only the manifest incoherence of dreams necessitated the postulation of the existence of an order of unconscious mentation that differs in fundamental ways from the manifest coherence of consciousness. Aspects of dreaming that resemble waking thoughts provide no necessary evidence of the *Ucs.*, and so played no role in Freud's argument. Only a categorical distinction between the types of thinking done by the *Ucs.* and *Pcpt.-Cs.* could furnish necessary reason to postulate the existence of the *Ucs.* Freud was concerned to mount a persuasive argument without dissipating its force by raising the moot issue of "the ostensible activity of the function of judgment." His polemical purpose led him, however, into the error of an argument *ex silencio*. Freud did not know that the unconscious dream-work cannot produce coherent thinking. All that he knew was that he could not prove the existence of the unconscious if it does.

Freud's failure to revise dream theory in perspective of the structural hypothesis introduced a fundamental distortion within psychoanalytic theory that analysts have never addressed. There is an abundance of evidence in support of the theoretic option over-looked by Freud, that coherent thinking contributes importantly to the unconscious elaboration of wish-fulfillments.

Punishment Dreams

With the superego identified as the agency responsible for con-science, Freud (1923c) was able to solve the long-standing puzzle of punishment dreams. He explained punishment dreams as reaction-formations that conscience induced.

> In . . . [punishment] dreams we are met by the remarkable fact that actually nothing belonging to the latent dream-thoughts is taken up into the manifest content of the dream. Something quite different appears instead, which must be described as a reaction-formation against the dream-thoughts, a rejection and complete contradiction of them. Such offensive action as this against the dream can only be ascribed to the critical agency of the ego [i.e., the superego] and it must there-fore be assumed that the latter, provoked by the unconscious wish-fulfilment, has been temporarily re-established even during the sleeping state (p. 118; cf. pp. 119, 132–33).

Punishment dreams have their basis in unconscious psycho-sexual materials whose manifestation would be pleasurable but morally objectionable. Because the materials are pleasurable, they are not subject to exclusion from consciousness through repression. The psyche is forced to rely on its other censorship of dreams, the censure of conscience; and a punishment dream ensues. For ex-ample, a wish to engage in morally objectionable sex may manifest in a dream that portrays the sexual activity, but portrays it with censure as dismaying. In such cases, Freud maintained that the censure of conscience occurs only after the objectionable material manifests, as a reaction or response to the dream. The argument was inconclusive but tenable. In the case of punishment dreams, however, the censure of conscience both responds to the uncon-scious wish and itself undergoes symbolization, displacing or re-placing the initial wish-fulfillment. To continue the same example, the manifest content of a punishment dream might portray neither the immoral sexual activity nor its pleasurability, but only some other activity that is censured with negative emotion. The manifest dream then amounts to a punishment for a wish that remains wholly unconscious. Recourse to displacement is so very complete that nothing manifests of the latent wish. "The essential characteristic of punishment-dreams would . . . be that in their case the dream-constructing wish is not an unconscious wish . . . but a punitive one reacting against it" (Freud, 1900, p. 558). Punishment dreams acquire their distinctive character through the recasting of provisional dream-contents in response to conscience (cf. Alexander, in Rangell, 1956, pp. 124–25). Moral censure of the wish motivates (and so necessarily occurs prior to) the unconscious displacement of the wished-for activity.

Anxiety Dreams

Evidence of unconscious wisdom in dreams is easily multiplied. On Freud's own showing, the fulfillments of wishes are not instantaneous but may instead undergo unconscious elaborations. Freud addressed the issue in connection with anxiety dreams in two paragraphs that he added to the 1919 edition of *The Interpretation of Dreams*.

> Dreams . . . with a distressing content may be either experienced with indifference, or they may be accompanied by the whole of the distressing affect which their ideational content seems to justify, or they may even lead to the development of anxiety and to awakening.
>
> Analysis is able to demonstrate that these unpleasurable dreams are wish-fulfilments no less than the rest. An unconscious and repressed wish, whose fulfilment the dreamer's ego could not fail to experience as something distressing, has seized the opportunity offered to it by the persisting cathexis of the distressing residues of the previous day; it has lent them its support and by that means rendered them capable of entering a dream (pp. 556–57).

This passage can be taken in two different senses. Why should some unconscious wishes be pleasurable and others distressing to consciousness? The passage offers a satisfactory account of anxiety dreams only if we understand Freud to have intended a distinction between wishes that are unconscious and wishes that are both "unconscious and repressed." An event is traumatic and its memory is subject to repression whenever it induces a paralyzing helplessness in consciousness (Freud, 1926). Such a memory always contains a conflict between the pleasure and the distress that were juxtaposed in the traumatic event. When a presently unsatisfied wish associates with a repressed memory, it associates with a wish whose past fulfillment was partly pleasurable, but partly distressing. The association initially proceeds with only half of the conflict. The presently unsatisfied wish associates with the past wish on the basis of its partly pleasurable fulfillment. It does not initially associate with the traumatic distress that the memory also contains. The conflict is revived, however, when the rest of the traumatic memory is employed in fantasying the fulfillment of the wish. French (1937a) explained: "The search of a drive for satisfaction will regularly be accompanied by a tendency to call up memories of previously unsuccessful attempts at satisfaction . . . the fulfilment of wishes . . . must also represent the unhappy consequences of wish-fulfilment" (p. 26).

Freud's theory of anxiety dreams takes for granted that the portrayal of a wish's fulfillment is a process that carefully observes temporal sequences. First is the association with the pleasurable component of a repressed memory. Only after the association begins to generate manifest symbolism of a pleasurable fulfillment does the further association with the traumatic element divert the dream into anxiety. Freud overlooked an important theoretic implication of this assumption. The sequential unfolding of the pleasurable and anxious elements of anxiety dreams cannot be reconciled with the temporal confusions within repressed memories unless we postulate the activity of an unconscious function that introduces an accurate temporal factor that repressed memories lack. If a dream starts pleasurably only to become anxious as it proceeds, even though the memory on which it was based was already anxiety-laden before the dream commenced, dream formation must include a factor or function that separates the pleasurable and anxious portions of conflicted memories and addresses the different portions in sequence.

The temporal function may most simply be associated with the superego, whose capacity to anticipate and signal the moral implications of future actions similarly presupposes a knowledge of time. "The superego functions from the viewpoint of a future ego, from the standpoint of the ego's future that is to be reached. . . . Conscience speaks to us from the viewpoint of an inner future" (Loewald, 1962, pp. 45, 46). "The superego embodies hopes, ideals, and aspirations for the future—that is not only its function but its nature" (Loevinger, 1976, p. 295). Although time perception is generally considered an ego function, the temporal valuation of behavior as early, timely, tardy, and so forth has conventionally been attributed to the superego (Oberndorf, 1941; Dooley, 1941; Bergler & Róheim, 1946). Because the superego's capacity to evaluate time presupposes its knowledge or perception of time, the superego evidently engages in time perception on a routine basis and may presumably continue to do so on occasions when the ego cannot. Schilder and Kauders (1926) cited awakening at a precise time as an instance of the superego's function as the sleep vigil.

Words in Dreams

Like punishment dreams and anxiety dreams, the use of language in dreams is inconsistent with Freud's allegation that the unconscious dream-work is wholly independent of "the function of judgment." In order to account for words in dreams, Freud (1900) argued that "all that the dream has done is to extract from the dream-thoughts fragments of speeches which have really been made or heard" (p. 418). Language can manifest in dreams only if the dream-work borrows memories of linguistic usage by the secondary process. This circumstance governs "such speeches in dreams as possess something of the sensory quality of speech, and which are described by the dreamer himself as being speeches" (p. 419). Language that dreamers experience as "merely thoughts such as occur in our waking thought-activity" originate in waking thought "and are often carried over unmodified into our dreams" (p. 420) without undergoing symbolization at all. Freud failed to recognize that his formulation makes it necessary to credit the dream-work with a capacity to integrate borrowed words in knowing and meaningful manners. Heynick (1981) commented:

If on the basis of specimens, dream-speech shows itself to be not only highly grammatical, but also often of impressive complexity, must it then be assumed that the verbal language faculty, by definition a logico-grammatical—and therefore 'secondary'—process, functions with no greater hindrance in dreams than in waking life? . . . if . . . 'splicing' and 'editing' has been carried out on the memory 'tapes', their recombining in a syntactically grammatical fashion must, after all, rely on some linguistic competence (pp. 304–5; cf. Heynick, 1993).

Heynick understated the argument. With the lone exception of inventing a word, all linguistic performance consists of precisely such a reutilization of borrowed language. The recombining of remembered words in dreams is precisely the same cognitive function that occurs in waking consciousness. Whether the psycholinguist Noam Chomsky (Lyons, 1977) is correct that linguistic ability depends on a "generative grammar" that is both unconscious and inborn, the use of words in dreams is consistent with Lacan's generalization that the unconscious is structured like a language.

The occurrence of visual puns in dreams is equally decisive. A dream's manifest content may portray something that, when expressed in words, becomes coherent as a pun whose second meaning belongs to the latent dream content (Yazmajian, 1968). Freud failed to recognize, however, that the dream-work cannot produce a visual pun unless it has sufficient lexical competence to play on words. And since the lexical competence is integral to the unconscious process of symbol-formation, it cannot plausibly be attributed to preconscious thought prior to sleep.

Isakower (1954) maintained that "speech elements in dreams are a direct contribution from the superego to the manifest content of the dream" (p. 3). He argued that spoken words that comment on the manifest dreams exhibit the superego's function of self-observation. Isakower assumed the validity of Freud's account of secondary elaboration, however, and took for granted that the superego's verbal contributions are made preconsciously prior to sleep. Baudry (1974) instead credited the dreaming psyche with the normal range of superego activities. He asserted "that the superego is continually active and present, though in altered form, during the entire process, all the way from the formation of the unconscious wish (repression), to the dream-work (censorship, distortion), secondary revision, and finally, the forgetting of dreams" (p. 585). Baudry recognized, however, that not all spoken words comment on the action in dreams. Although spoken words in some cases expressed reproaches that were consistent with the superego's function of conscience, in other cases there were no apparent criteria for attributing the words to the superego. Some dreams "seem to consist almost entirely of *conversations*" (p. 599) and "have a structure similar to waking fantasies or daydreams" (p. 601).

The Rationality of Symbolization

Further evidence of rationality in the dream-work was advanced by Jean Piaget. For Freud's purposes in 1900, it sufficed to assert that condensation and displacement occur and are irrational processes. The reasons for their occurrence were unnecessary to Freud's argument that the very occurrence of irrationality required the postulation of the unconscious. This argument necessitates a different presentation today, among other reasons because Freud's later work rendered obsolete the prepsychoanalytic understanding of irrationality that he took for granted in 1900. Freud wrote *The Interpretation of Dreams* for readers who accepted a categorical distinction between reason and irrationality, without need for further discussion. Through Freud we have come to expect explanations, because he taught us to understand that irrationality invariably has a logic of its own. "The whole enterprise of interpreting dreams, delusions, and other baffling forms of pathological cognition is based on the premise of a hidden order in apparent disorder, which is the essential 'method in madness'" (Holt, 1967a, p. 351).

Freud's formulations permit no other conclusion. If every symbol in every dream has a latent meaning that differs from its manifest content, every symbol is a metaphor. Some symbols are evident to consciousness as metaphors. Others are not. In the latter cases, the goal of psychoanalytic dream interpretation is to alert consciousness of the latent metaphoricity of the dream images. Metaphoricity exists unconsciously in all events. Symbols that are not self-evidently metaphoric are metaphors whose latent contents exist but happen to be unconscious. Because metaphors are inherently rational phenomena, symbolization must be considered a rational process.

Piaget (1951) attempted to be more specific:

> In spite of its apparent lack of coherence, symbolic thought contains an element of logic, a pre-logic of a level comparable to intuitive pre-logic . . . condensation, like generalisation, involves giving a common meaning to a number of distinct objects, thus making it possible to give expression to a nest of affective schemas assimilating to one another various situations which are often widely separated in time . . . in the realm of images and affective assimilations displacement corresponds to abstraction in the realm of thought (p. 210).

Piaget maintained that condensation and displacement manipulate concrete representations in the same manner that generalization and abstraction work with conceptual thoughts.

Freud presented condensation and displacement as axioms of his theory of dream-work; but the two types of symbol-formation should not be treated as exceptions to Freud's methodological paradigm that irrationality is to be interpreted as a logical mental operation by reconstructing its unconscious assumptions.

Condensation and displacement are fantasies, but neither is a random consequence of "unbound energy" or "free cathexis" such as Freud thought them to be. Condensation expresses the idea of logical equivalence in the form of a metaphor. Like the adaptive metaphors (Silberer, 1912; Merkur, 1988) used in scientific thinking, condensation is a means of expressing a rational concept. Every condensation expresses a *tertium quid*, a point of comparison that is an independent or third entity mediating between the two mental elements being condensed. The point of comparison may be their lowest common denominator, or highest common factor, or any other commonality. Every condensation is both a *generalization* and, in the general sense of the term, a derivative or *abstraction*. In every case, the point of comparison is a synergic concept—an idea that neither contributor to the condensation expressed on its own, that came into being only through their union, as an expression of their union. For example, if a dream condenses the image of an orange with that of a lemon, the combined image implies a point of comparison, such as the concept of a citrus fruit. The condensation, or combined image, is the signifier;

what is signified is the point of comparison between the mental elements being condensed. Initially, the concept represented by the signified has no other means of conceptualization than the condensation and can only be expressed in metaphor. It is only later that a word may be invented in order to name the point of comparison.

Displacement is a compromise between condensation and censorship. Unconsciously, condensation and displacement are the same process. However, condensation manifests as displacement whenever part of the condensed materials is barred from consciousness. To continue the same example, should the idea of a lemon be repressed, a dream will be able to manifest only part of the condensation—that is, the image of an orange. The image of the lemon is then said to be displaced by the image of the orange. Importantly, the general idea of a citrus fruit will still be attached to the manifest image, an orange, but for no manifest reason.

To conclude, condensation is a rational process. Displacement is responsible for manifest irrationality, but only out of compromise with repression. The unconscious meaning of every displacement is always a condensation—and rational.

Two Types of Latent Contents

Armed with the conclusive example of punishment dreams, Freud might have generalized that the superego's contributions to dreams frequently or regularly occur unconsciously. He preferred, however, to perpetuate his initial equation of dreaming and symbolization. Freud presumably failed to notice his oversight because a systematic inconsistency had crept into his practice of dream interpretation.

Freud (1900) initially asserted that the manifest images of dreams conceal latent contents that pertain to unsatisfied wishes of recent conscious experience. Freud's *Three Essays on the Theory of Sexuality* (1905b) implied the existence of latent concerns that were unremitting, psychosexual, and repressed. Because Freud neglected to provide appropriate terminological distinctions, few psychoanalytic writers have ever appreciated that the manifest images of dreams have two different sorts of latent content. Ernest Jones and Robert Fliess were notable exceptions. Jones (1928) contrasted "metaphors, emblems, similes, and so on, in fact almost any process in which one idea stands for another," which are symbolic in the popular sense of the term, with the technical meaning of symbolism in psychoanalysis, which "designate[s] a peculiar process whereby an idea or process represents an associated one which is in a state of repression in the unconscious mind" (p. 10). Single images may have two levels of latent meaning simultaneously. For example, in the case of "the custom of throwing rice at weddings . . . psycho-analysts would say that rice is an *emblem* of fertility, but a *symbol* of seed" (p. 11). Fliess (1973) suggested that the meanings of emblems are *"conscious and dependent upon having learned them"* while "the use of the analytic symbol is *unconscious and independent of learning"* (p. 7). The suggestion is untenable, however. Some symbols, whose meanings as metaphors arc evident immediately upon their manifestation, emerge from the unconscious to express ideas that have never previously been attained (Silberer, 1912; Merkur, 1988a). The distinction between emblems and symbols arises from the mode and context of a motif's interpretation. The same rice that is an emblem of fertility at a wedding is simultaneously a symbol of seed in the context of the bridal couple's psychosexuality. The id treats as a symbol whatever reality-testing and metaphor-formation combine to treat as an emblem.

Neither the symbolic nor the emblematic meaning of dreams is manifest. Rice, for example, is manifestly rice. It does not manifestly mean either fertility or seed. Because the emblematic significance of a motif is no more manifest than the symbolic, the images of dreams have always two types or orders of meaning that are genuinely latent and unconscious. As a rule, the emblematic level is latent because at least part of it has never before manifested. With a little effort, however, the dreamer's associations will readily lead to coherent interpretation of the emblematic content of the dream. The symbolic level, by contrast, is latent because at least part of it is repressed and cannot become conscious.

Freud's preoccupation with psychosexuality and the therapy of psychopathology led him to neglect the emblematic level of dreams' interpretations. The systematic oversight was already in force in *The Interpretation of Dreams*, where Freud (1900) hinted at the sexual theories that he was then in process of formulating.

There is often a passage in even the most thoroughly interpreted dream which has to be left obscure; this is because we become aware during the work of interpretation that at that point there is a tangle of dream-thoughts which cannot be unravelled and which moreover adds nothing to our knowledge of the content of the dream. This is the dream's navel, the spot where it reaches down into the unknown. The dream-thoughts to which we are led by interpretation cannot, from the nature of things, have any definite endings; they are bound to branch out in every direction into the intricate net-work of our world of thought. It is at some point where this meshwork is particularly close that the dream-wish grows up, like a mushroom out of its mycelium (p. 525; cf. p. 111, n. 1).

In psychoanalyzing a dream, it is appropriate to commence with the emblematic order of meanings, in order to learn what a dream has symbolized. Only after the latent dream-thoughts, with their presently unsatisfied wish, have been reconstructed with the aid of the dreamers' associations (see Langs, 1988; 1991; 1994b), does it become appropriate to ask why the latent dream-thoughts have been symbolized in the manner that the dream has employed— why certain images were chosen for use as emblems. In this task, the dreamers' associations invariably fail eventually; and the evidence of resistance is, for methodological purposes, psychoanalysis's warrant for postulating a fundamentally different order of meaning—one that is symbolic, rather than emblematic. A dreamer's associations pertain to the latent dream-thoughts, which, Freud claimed, are invariably coherent (as emblems) in the context of the dreamers' waking life and conscious concerns. It is only the second order of interpretation, the analyst's insight concerning the resistance to free association, that pertains to the symbolism of unconscious instinctual desires.

It is customary in psychoanalytic training and clinical practice to slight the latent dream-thoughts while searching among an analysand's associations for evidence of resistance. Sharpe's *Dream Analysis* (1937) went so far as to advise analysts to ignore the emblematic order of meaning, which she mistakenly called "the manifest content" (p. 79). The therapeutic short-cut is at best a compromise in deference to limitations of time. However, neither a complete interpretation nor a complete theory of dreams may privilege the particular data that happen to be valued by a particular technique of therapy.

Freud's restriction of the dream-work to symbolization was persuasive only because he limited his clinical practice of dream interpretation, so far as possible, to the analysis of dreams' psychosexual significances. Had he taken an equal interest in dreams' pertinence to the unsatisfied wishes of dreamers' conscious lives, he would have encountered the dreams' practical relevance to daily events and rapidly recognized the unconscious superego's contributions. His theory of the Oedipal etiology of neurosis monopolized his clinical technique; and because his clinical technique was skewed, it skewed the evidence that emerged in his consulting room, in a fashion that seemed to support his theory.

French and Fromm's Theory of Problem-Solving

To the 1914 edition of *The Interpretation of Dreams*, Freud (1900) added a paragraph in which he endorsed Ferenczi's view that dreams engage in problem-solving.

> Ferenczi . . . remarks: 'Dreams work over the thoughts which are occupying the mind at the moment from every angle; they will drop a dream-image if it threatens the success of a wish-fulfilment and will experiment with a fresh solution, till at last they succeed in constructing a wish-fulfilment which satisfies both agencies of the mind as a compromise.' (p. 572).

Ferenczi's notion of solving the problem of symbol-formation must be contrasted, however, with theories that dreams solve the practical problems of dreamers' lives. Freud (1900, pp. 524, 579 n. 1) rejected the formulations of Adler (1936), Maeder (1916), and Silberer ([1918] 1955). Because the theories pertained to manifest dreams, they implied that dreams possess a manifest coherence that they manifestly do not. If symbolization were limited to considerations of representability and condensation, manifest dreams would be coherent, because they would be consistent with Silberer's (1912) findings on "auto-symbolic" phenomena in hypnagogic reveries. Unlike waking fantasies, however, dreams take extensive recourse to displacements, and their coherence is an artifact of interpretation.

Related methodological objections may be raised to ego psychological studies of the manifest dream by Erikson (1954), R. M. Jones (1962; 1969; 1970), and many others (Leavitt, 1957; Ullman, 1959; 1961; Snyder, 1966; Hawkins, 1966; Ephron & Carrington, 1967; Nell, 1968; Dewan, 1970; Pearlman, 1970; Fosshage, 1983; 1987), including proponents of information-processing models of the psyche (Breger, 1969; Greenberg & Pearlman, 1975; 1978; Palombo, 1978; Greenberg, 1981; 1987; Cartwright, 1986). After demonstrating that dreams make use of rational ideas, these writers explained the presence of rationality by postulating ego activity during sleep. The theoretic option is not available, however. The unconscious rationality of dreams cannot be attributed to the ego, because the ego's inactivity is responsible for dreams' hallucinatory quality.

The ego's inactivity is readily demonstrated. The hallucinations and delusions of dreams, hypnosis, and psychopathology have the quality of seeming real. The hallucinations and delusions seem real for the simple reason that fantasies have no intrinsic quality that differs from the realism of sensations, perceptions, and their memories. All fantasies initially possess a quality of seeming real. As long as their reality is not tested and falsified, fantasies cannot be recognized as fictions. They instead have a "psychic reality" (Freud, 1916–17) that is able, for example, to provoke the unconscious guilt that would be appropriate for the behaviors imagined. Freud (1911, p. 222; 1930, p. 80) suggested that children's play, daydreaming, and the illusions of art and religion retain the quality of the real because they are exempt from refutation by reality-testing. A theory of hallucination may be developed by extending the same line of reasoning. Whenever reality-testing is suspended or inhibited, fantasies cannot be falsified. They can only be experienced uncritically as though they concerned realities. Immunity from falsification is the hallmark of hallucinations and delusions. Inhibitions of reality-testing vary in extent and are never complete. They may arise in any of several manners. In the case of dreaming, the reality-testing process simply goes to sleep. The gradual shading of hypnagogic fantasies from pseudo-hallucinations into hallucinations (Mavromatis, 1987) is due, I suggest, to the progressive relaxation of reality-testing. The awakening of reality-testing produces the reversed sequence of events in hypnopompic fantasies. Because the ego's reality-testing function is mutually exclusive with dreams' hallucinatory quality, we have reason to doubt that the sleeping ego remains sufficiently active to produce the occasional rationality of manifest dreams.

Most other approaches to the manifest dream add little of present pertinence. Even as sophisticated a formulation as Breger's (1969) account of "the adaptive function of dreams" unwittingly stated as a new discovery what Freud had always contended regarding the unsatisfied present wish of the dreamer. Breger wrote:

> Dreams serve to integrate affectively aroused material into structures within the memory systems that have previously proved satisfactory in dealing with similar materials.
>
> These may be purely defensive solutions (all rationalization, no accomplishment), magical solutions, or solutions with a large reality component (pp. 218–19).

Freud would have added that dreams' success and failure at attempted adaptations are chance by-products of wish-fulfillment. In Freud's view, dreams' portraits of the fulfillment of wishes sometimes provide practical solutions and sometimes do not. For example, Freud (1900) treated the repetitive dreams of traumatic neurosis as evidence that some dreams facilitate the mastery of traumatic materials (see also Fenichel, 1945; Garma, 1946; Bonaparte, 1947; Loewenstein, 1949; Ward, 1961; Stein, 1965; Stewart, 1967; Greenberg, Pearlman, & Gampel, 1972; Greenberg, Pillard, & Pearlman, 1972; Myers, 1983; 1989).

From Adler through contemporary dream research, few existing arguments concerning the problem-solving function of dreaming meet the methodological standards maintained and demanded by Freud. A notable exception was offered in a series of publications by Thomas M. French (1937b; 1939; 1952; 1954; 1957; 1970) and his co-workers (Fromm & French, 1962; French & Fromm, 1964; French & Whitman, 1969). French's arguments remain cogent and persuasive. French (1937b) began with the clinical observation that the interpretations of analysands' dreams sometimes disclose solutions to emotional and behavioral problems, days or weeks before the analysands are willing consciously to embrace the same insights. French concluded that "the dream has been able to achieve a solution for a conflict that waking thought is still quite unable to solve. The dream-work is, by several weeks or even months, cleverer than waking thought" (p. 65). French was initially unable to decide whether the wisdom of the dream was an unconscious part of the dream-work, or had been achieved preconsciously during the previous day.

Fifteen years later, French (1952) published an argument that was conclusive but incomplete. He argued that the unsatisfied wish that belongs to the day's residue may be considered not only in the conventional clinical manner by reference to infantile sexual wishes, but also in relation to the censorship. When the wish is so examined, the censorship proves to critique the wish not by rote, but with rational intelligence. "The dream censor turns out to be not an impersonal system of the mind but a specific inhibitory motive, an appropriate reaction to this particular wish" (p. 70).

Like Freud, French emphasized the positive contributions of the censorship.

The inhibiting motive plays not only a censoring role but also a creative role in shaping the fantasy activity that culminates in the manifest dream. The dreamer's pride, threatened by a dependent wish, may react with compensatory fantasies of independence and achievement or may try to conjure up a situation in which the dependent craving would not be too incompatible with self-respect. The dreamer whose guilt has been aroused by his hostile wishes may imagine himself unjustly treated in order to justify his hostility; or his guilt may demand appeasement by a fantasy of being punished (pp. 71–72).

The dream, French asserted, does not consist of "isolated fragments of a tangle of latent dream thoughts . . . being displaced along any available associative pathway." Instead, the dream-work may be seen to be "struggling somehow to reconcile these two conflicting motives" (p. 72). French (1954) suggested that the reconstruction of the latent dream-content should be followed by an attempt to understand the nature of the conflict between the unsatisfied wish of the day's residue and the "reactive motive" of the censorship.

> There is usually a problem from which all the dream wishes radiate. This we call the *focal problem or focal conflict (FC)* of the dream. . . . *The focal problem*, since it is the problem with which the dreamer is unconsciously preoccupied at the moment of dreaming, *is always anchored in the present* (p. 26).

Once interpretation has identified the dream's focal conflict, it becomes possible to reconstruct the logical steps by which the dream-work distorted the latent content in order to satisfy the censorship. The dream-work would then be found to be "dominated by the need to find a solution for a problem" (p. 15). "The problem is to find a way in real life to reconcile the dreamer's disturbing motive and his reactive motive" (French, 1957, p. 256).

Among the many illustrations that French provided for his thesis was a reinterpretation of a dream that Freud had discussed in "Fragment of an analysis of a case of hysteria" (1905a). Freud's patient Dora had reported the following dream.

> *A house was on fire. My father was standing beside my bed and woke me up. I dressed quickly. Mother wanted to stop and save her jewel-case; but Father said: "I refuse to let myself and my two children be burnt for the sake of your jewel-case." We hurried downstairs, and as soon as I was outside I woke up* (p. 64).

Dora, who was eighteen, had been vacationing with her father at the home of a Mr. and Mrs. K. The dream occurred three times, on the second, third, and fourth nights after Dora had rejected Mr. K.'s sexual proposition. Dora's associations clarified some of the motifs in her dream. When Dora and her father had first arrived at Mr. K.'s house, her father had spoken of his fear that the wooden structure might catch fire (p. 65). The motif of her father standing beside her bed had been inspired by Mr. K.'s further attempts at seduction. Dora stated:

> In the afternoon after our trip on the lake, from which we (Herr K. and I) returned at midday, I had gone to lie down as

usual on the sofa in the bedroom to have a short sleep. I suddenly awoke and saw Herr K. standing beside me. . . . This episode put me on my guard, and I asked Frau K. whether there was not a key to the bedroom door. The next morning I locked myself in while I was dressing. That afternoon, when I wanted to lock myself in so as to lie down again on the sofa, the key was gone. I was convinced that Herr K. had removed it. . . . On the subsequent mornings I could not help feeling afraid that Herr K. would surprise me while I was dressing: *so I always dressed very quickly* (pp. 66–67).

The jewel-case had two associations for Dora. Her first response was that "Mother is very fond of jewelry and had had a lot given her by Father" (p. 68). Dora also acknowledged that "Herr K. had made me a present of an expensive jewel-case a little time before" (p. 69).

Freud treated Dora's memories of Mr. K.'s attempts at seduction as the day's residue in the dream. The dream, Freud interpreted, reflected Dora's feelings that she could get no quiet sleep as long as she remained in Mr. K.'s house (p. 67). "The intention might have been consciously expressed in some such words as these: 'I must fly from this house, for I see that my virginity is threatened here; I shall go away with my father, and I shall take precautions not to be surprised while I am dressing in the morning'" (p. 85). The dream also reflected other trends of Dora's thought. The fire symbolized her sexual desire for Mr. K. The jewel-case symbolized her genitals. The dream repressed Dora's sexual desire for Mr. K. by invoking her childhood love for her father (p. 70). Freud suggested that Dora's expressions "an accident might happen in the night" and "it might be necessary to leave the room" were coherent in terms of bed-wetting. Her father's role in awakening her out of sleep was consistent with precautions against bed-wetting. From the dream's representation of her father referring to his "two children," Freud inferred that both Dora and her brother "were addicted to bed-wetting up to a later age than is usual with children" (p. 72). Dora confirmed that her brother had been so. In her own case, however, she had learned continence but had temporarily reverted to bed-wetting at an age of seven or eight.

To Freud's interpretation, French added several observations. French (1954) suggested that the focal conflict of Dora's dream was the "conflict between her waking resolution to leave the house with her father and her temptation to stay behind and accept Mr. K.'s sexual advances" (p. 14). This conflict was displaced through projection as a conflict between her father and her mother regarding the jewel-case. The projection satisfied the censorship by effacing all references to Dora's lust and substituting the motifs of fire and the jewel-case. The projection of Dora's reluctance to leave onto her mother, and of her desire to leave onto her father, also provided her with emotional distance from her conflict (pp. 14–17). French regarded emotional detachment from a conflict as a frequent device of dreams; it sometimes provides sufficient perspective for insight to ensue. Projection both avoids distress and is "a technique of intellectual mastery" (French, 1957, p. 247). French emphasized that the dream-work had not proceeded through arbitrary and irrational associations as Freud had claimed. "The dream censor acts not in response to only one motive, but in the service of the problem-solving function of the dreamer's ego" (p. 246).

Freud's theories have as their logical corollary what French took as his general thesis: that the positive contributions of the dream-censorship have a purposive, problem-solving function that mediates between the unsatisfied wish of the day's residue and the reactive motive of the censorship. Freud plainly erred in assuming that rational thought can make no unconscious contributions to the formation of dreams. The recasting of provisional dream-contents is not only theoretically possible; on French's showing it is a routine feature of symbol-formation.

French's position dovetails with my own. When symbolization is understood as a process of translation that expresses coherent ideas in forms that the primary process can access, condensation and displacement cease to appear as irrational processes. The symbols that they produce may be irrational, but the processes themselves are rational.

Because the manifest rationality of secondary revisions differs markedly from the latent rationality of symbol-formation through condensation and displacement, the two processes may not immediately be equated. There are good reasons, however, for making the equation. The revised version of his theory that French developed together with Erika Fromm persuasively argued that problem-solving is performed *both before and after* the production of symbols.

French and Fromm (1964) emphasized that the manifestation of an unconscious symbol diverts the course of the manifest dream from its original topic "to analogues or related, but less disturbing problems" and then proceeds to address the analogues (p. 179). In Dora's dream, for example, the interaction of her mother and father follows the dream-work's displacement of her sexuality through the motifs of fire and the jewel-case. Their interaction was manifestly coherent. The dream characters discussed the interrelations of the fire, a jewel-case, and children's lives. Because the motifs of the mother and father originated through unconscious displacement, the rationality of the two character's discussion in the dream may be recognized as an instance of "secondary revision." The problem-solving that was responsible for the manifest dream's "secondary revision" must have been produced after the displacement occurred, but before the dream concluded with the family fleeing the burning house. French and Fromm (1964) wrote:

> Part of the time [t]he [dreamer] is trying to find a solution for his conflict. When the problem threatens to become too difficult or disturbing, he withdraws from it and focuses his interest on a similar but less disturbing problem. Even after he has withdrawn in this way, however, he continues his problem-solving effort, trying to find a solution for the problem that has been substituted . . . the *defensive maneuver* [of symbolization] has been *subordinated* to the attempt at *problem-solving*. The dream-work has substituted an easier problem and then continued with its problem-solving effort (pp. 66–67).

French and Fromm's suggestion that a latent attempt at problem-solving is a universal feature of dreams has been accepted by some writers (Hawkins, 1966; Noy, 1969). French and Fromm are sometimes taken to have offered a theory of the manifest dream, but their findings are then misunderstood. Contentions that the manifest dream facilitates working through (Greenacre, 1956), seeks mastery over conflicts in the day residue (Stewart, 1967), is consistent with the purposes and nature of waking thought (Spanjaard, 1969), or has an adaptive function (Palombo, 1978) commonly overlook the manifest dream's deflection from these alleged functions through the intrusion of unconscious symbols. French claimed that rational problem-solving by the dream-work mediates between the unsatisfied wish in the latent dream-content and the reactive motive of the dream-censorship. French and Fromm added that the deflection of problem-solving in the manifest dream proves that the problem-solving is performed not only before but also during the dreaming. It is not necessarily part of the day's residue as the topographic model had led Freud to insist.

The Prognostic Function of Conscience

In refuting Freud's claim of the invariable irrationality of dream-work, French limited his arguments to dream-work as Freud had defined it: condensation, displacement, and considerations of representability. French proved his case that dream-work includes rational thought when he demonstrated that the manifest dream is a failed attempt at problem-solving. Dreams are able to engage in problem-solving only because rational thinking plays a role in the unconscious dream-work. The problem-solving generally fails, however, because dream-work includes irrational elements. The dream-work's rational thinking is not a merely secondary revision. It occurs both before and after symbolization. Since dreams frequently contain several symbols, and the problem-solving addresses each in its turn, it is evident that the dream-work's rational thinking occurs in alternation with symbolization. It is not limited to the preconscious elaboration of the day's residue in advance of sleep or to the waking ego's responses to dream's manifestation as a whole. The rational thinking is an integral part of the unconscious dream-work.

French and Fromm were content to refute Freud by demonstrating rational attempts to reconcile the dreamer's disturbing motive and his reactive motive. They did not go on to establish what these failed attempts at problem-solving accomplish. They attributed the problem-solving to the dream censorship, but they questioned the adequacy of conventional superego theories to account for reactive motives other than guilt (p. 92). French (1952) noted the practical orientation of the dream-work's intelligence. "It is . . . thinking in terms of the practical grasp of real situations: 'If I act upon this wish, then I must expect such and such consequences. Shall I renounce the wish or suffer the consequences? Or is some compromise possible?' " (p. 72). French and Fromm (1964, p. 92) contrasted the dream-work's interpersonal concerns with the logical thinking of the secondary process. "In most cases, the dreamer's thinking is struggling with concrete, practical problems involving his relationship to other people" (p. 86).

It is my contention that the latent problem-solving of dreams is regularly successful. French and Fromm thought it unsuccessful only because they equated success with a reconciliation of the dreamer's wish and reactive motive. I agree that the problem-solving addresses the unsatisfied wish in the light of the censorship's reactive motive, but I emphasize the role that conscience plays in the process. In depicting a wish as fulfilled, the process of symbolization does not think through the real logical consequences of the wish's fulfillment. The dream-censorship nevertheless does so. Whether the superego's prognosis is favorable or not, the dream-work invariably succeeds in formulating a judgment of conscience.

In Dora's dream, for example, her sexuality was symbolized twice. As fire that was destroying the house, her sexuality was evidently bad, for it had to be fled. As a jewel-case that her mother desired to save, Dora's sexuality was implicitly good. The contexts of the two sexual motifs are telling. In the dream, Dora acquired her knowledge of the fire that must be fled when her father stood over her bed as Mr. K. had done. Importantly, the real Dora was able to interpret this motif on the basis of her conscious associations. Repression was not the type of censorship that required the displacement of Mr. K. as Dora's father. Dora was similarly able consciously to connect the dream motif of dressing quickly with her actual practice of dressing quickly to avoid Mr. K. The sexuality that Dora had to flee may be interpreted by reference to its disguised but unrepressed associations with Mr. K. The dream urged Dora to flee sex with Mr. K. The substitution of Dora's father for Mr. K. standing over her bed meant that sex with Mr. K. was as improper as sex with her father.

The motif of the jewel-case differed. In the dream, it was not Dora but her mother who wanted the jewel-case. In her associations, Dora connected the motif with her mother's liking for jewels before she remembered that Mr. K. had once given her (Dora) a jewel-case. The sequence of associations indicates that Dora's mother was a displacement of herself. Once again, the symbol was disguised but its meaning was not repressed. What was being said in this manifestly metaphoric manner? That sexual desire was virtuous for Dora when she was Mother—implicitly, when she would be lawfully wed to a husband, as her mother was. The dream's verbal reference to "my two children" alluded still more clearly to the concept of a couple. For the same reason, it was Father—now signifying Dora's future husband—who hurried the family out of the burning house.

Nothing that was necessary to the moral interpretation of Dora's dream was repressed. Much was distorted, but nothing was repressed. This observation agrees approximately with the view of R. M. Jones (1965; 1969; 1970a; 1970b), who suggested that the very notions of disguise, distortion, and censorship are misnomers for what is actually a process of transformation. Where Freud considered symbolization to be an evasive response to repression and the superego's censorship, French and Fromm demonstrated that symbolization reconciles the unsatisfied wish with the dream-censorship. Since the censorship knows the latent content, Jones concluded that the purpose of symbolization cannot be to conceal latent content from the dream-censorship. He maintained that the dream-forming process is not adequately described as a censorship, because symbolization originates as a fully comprehensible correction, revision, or improvement of the latent content. His suggestion is valid, in my opinion, for the emblematic level of the dream's meaning, its moral or existential content, but not for all of its meaning "from below."

In Dora's dream, the distortions provided metaphoric commentaries on the latent dream-content that treated it as a moral dilemma and evaluated its different parts. For the same reason, I cannot endorse the view of Jekels and Bergler (1940) that the censure of conscience is added to the latent contents during preconscious elaboration of the day's residue, prior to sleep. *The judgments of conscience are expressed through the dream-work's choice of symbols.* Its occurrence cannot be demonstrated apart from symbol-formation. In other words, *the process of symbolization is a superego function.*

In no case can any of the distortions in Dora's dream be shown to be responses to repression. The chief repressions were two. Freud was only eventually able to get Dora to consent to his interpretation of childhood bed-wetting, and she remained utterly unimpressed by his suggestions that she had harbored sexual desires in childhood for her father. If we assume that Freud was correct and Dora resisted interpretations that were valid, we may conclude that the dream-work had access to repressed memories of infantile sexuality. If so, it utilized repressed materials in precisely the same manner that it accomplished latent but unrepressed problem-solving. However, the determination as to what unconscious reasoning was to be repressed, and what permitted to manifest, was not made by the dream-work. It was instead made by the ego's stimulus barriers after the dream-work had been performed.

Interpreted in this manner as a dream "from above" as well as "from below," Dora's dream may be recognized as a detailed and coherent analysis of her moral sensibilities. The dream clarified to Dora how she truly felt. When Mr. K. propositioned her, she had been outraged. Freud (1905a) reported that "no sooner had she grasped Herr K.'s intention than, without letting him finish what he had to say, she had given him a slap in the face and hurried away" (p. 46). Elsewhere Freud referred to "the insult to her honour" (p. 26) and "her pride" (p. 58); but the dream reveals moral considerations that were less superficial. They belonged not to her social persona, her false self, but to her true self. At the time of Mr. K.'s proposition, she had consciously felt only an insult to her honor. Why had she not felt anything more? Presumably because she had not allowed herself to acknowledge the further feelings that the dream revealed. The dream indicated that her feelings were mixed, and it resolved her ambivalence into its components. The dream's images indicate that Dora was flattered by Mr. K's attention, and perhaps sexually attracted to him. But she also wanted to flee him, because in her view sex was virtuous only in the context of marriage. In this way, the dream expressed the decision of her unconscious conscience to postpone sex until marriage.

Because the emotions in dreams reflect the latent content (Freud, 1900), Dora's feelings were self-evident to her when she awoke. Her associations to her feelings need not have permitted her to interpret all of her dream's symbolism for her to have successfully related the feelings to her ongoing waking circumstances. Her decision had been made while she dreamt, and enough of the dream's meaning was transparent that she acted on her decision when she awoke.

In functioning as a dream censorship, the unconscious super-ego does not approve or censure dreams as wholes, but undertakes judgmental analyses and explorations of dreams' individual parts. Each aspect of a dream is reinterpreted from the superego's perspective. Whatever self-interested thinking the provisional dream content inherited from the ego is reassessed in the light of conscience. The result is not only a wish's implementation but also a prognosis of the consequences of the wish's fulfillment. In many cases, a wish's real fulfillment would be unobjectionable; but in other cases, a real fulfillment, which the dreamer selfishly wishes to be pleasurable, would prove morally objectionable. The superego is able to anticipate and warn against some of the grief that the real pursuit of certain wishes would precipitate. The conclusion attained by the superego is invariably either to approve or disapprove of the wish. It is indicated at minimum by an emotion that reacts or responds to the fulfillment. The reactive emotion may be opposite to the initial emotion (cf. Brenner, 1973, p. 178). In Dora's dream, the fear of the fire was a reactive emotion. It contrasted with the wishful desire for the jewel-box. Reactive emotions and other superego materials function as signals that serve either to encourage or caution against efforts to secure the real satisfactions of wishes. The procedure is a kind of moral commentary; *it is also a kind of secondary revision*. The dream-work's rational thinking is not devoted to the problem of how an unsatisfied wish may be fulfilled in reality, much less how it might best be fulfilled. It assumes the wish's implementation for the sake of argument and then proceeds to develop a detailed prognosis of the moral consequences of the provisional wish-fulfillment.

The prognostic aspect of the superego's unconscious function is critical, I suggest, to a major use of dreaming in everyday life. "Dreaming serves to exercise man's unique capacity for self-perception in depth" (R. M. Jones, 1970a, p. 187). When a person "sleeps on" a problem as an aid to decision-making (Casey, 1943; Wolff, 1952, p. 283; Tauber & Green, 1959, pp. 171–72; Nell, 1968; Fiss, Klein, & Shollar, 1974, pp. 416–17), dreaming is used as a means less of problem-solving than of introspection. Dreams access unconscious desires, the repressed, and the value judgments of the unconscious superego, and so permit people to discover how they feel about decisions that they must make (cf. Kelman, 1975). In latent dream formation, "the unconscious system is not bent on immediate gratification but is capable of working through an emotional issue slowly, weighing all the factors involved; if anything, it is the conscious system that acts quickly" (Langs, 1988, p. 58).

French and Fromm's remarks on problem-solving by the dream-work do not pertain to the practical, impersonal problem-solving that is conventionally meant by "creativity" in the contexts of the arts and sciences. The problem-solving in dreams pertains to the process of coming to morally honest self-knowledge regarding the desirability of future actions. Creative inspirations may manifest during sleep (Lewin, 1958; 1962; E. Hartmann, 1973; 1976), but creativity and dreaming are best treated as independent variables. Creativity can occur during sleep as a stream of verbal ideation without undergoing the symbolization distinctive of dreaming. Creative inspiration is an infrequent and perhaps rare occurrence in dreams. Moral decision-making is instead integral to their nature.

Freud (1900; 1925b) raised the problem that many dreams have immoral contents. I suggest, however, that once allowance is made for differences among individuals' standards of morality, the immoral contents prove to belong to manifest dreams alone. The latent meanings of dreams other than anxiety dreams and the dreams of traumatic neurosis are invariably consistent with the dreamer's superego values. Because moral issues happened to be prominent in Dora's dream as well as in conventional views of the superego, I have constructed the argument of this chapter accordingly. However, the emotional value judgments in dreams are not restricted to moral questions.

Robert Langs (1988) found that when dreams are interpreted in terms of the recent events that "trigger" them, they regularly offer "deep unconscious wisdom."

Because the conscious system is designed for immediate action, it often misperceives, fails to see, or slants our view away from the most painful attributes or implications of a disturbing experience. It is in the deep unconscious system that we process the most painful and terrifying aspects of emotionally charged triggers—dimensions that the conscious system is not equipped to handle, either because they are too disturbing or too complicated and unlikely to issue in a direct and logical form of response. . . . The deep unconscious system is quite incisive and uncompromising in its thinking about . . . events and their implications. This reliable sense of certainty is one of the many advantages to dealing with an emotionally charged trigger event with knowledge of your unconscious picture of the situation. Deep unconscious processing is a far superior instrument of adaptation as compared to conscious processing. . . . [T]he unconscious system . . . is capable of working through an emotional issue slowly, weighing all the factors involved (pp. 39, 53, 58).

Because Langs chose to revise Freud's topographic hypothesis, with its dualistic model of *Pcpt.-Cs.* and the *Ucs.*, he attributed the wisdom of dreams to a "deep unconscious wisdom system, which effectively uses unconscious perception and a deep intelligence to receive unconsciously and to process incoming meaning and information" (1992, p. 9). "The deep unconscious system has its own values and its own intolerances, in that certain behaviors are experienced as quite contradictory and unacceptable" (1988, p. 59).

Langs' (1988) observations all pertain to what I conceptualize as unconscious superego activity.

This deep unconscious system silently works over and processes the charged information. It sorts out the elements of a hurtful situation, the nature of the threat, and suggests ways of handling the danger. But the information that is being processed is terrifying and cannot be experienced directly by the conscious mind. Because of this, most of the perceptions and working over of this type of potentially disturbing experience are conveyed indirectly through *transformed* or disguised images—such as those that occur in dreams (p. 92).

The superego contributes self-observations as well as value-judgments to dreams; and its values include questions not only of morality but also of etiquette, aesthetics, and so forth.

In attributing gaps in dreams to repression, and distortions in dreams to moralizing revisions by the dream-censorship, I have implied that most instances of the evasive function of displacement are required by neither of the processes that Freud offered in its explanation. A minority of displacements are required by repression; but the dream-censorship is so far from requiring displacement as to perform the majority of its instances. Why is dream distortion required? I am not prepared to follow theoreticians of the manifest dream (e.g., R. M. Jones, 1970a, 1970b) in arguing that there is no dream distortion, that dreams simply utilize a symbolic mode of expression. I claim only that Freud failed to recognize that every dream is a dream both "from above" and "from below," and that a dream is not fully interpreted until both orders of meaning have been exposed. A dream does not portray only the enactment of a wish; it portrays both the enactment and a value judgment on it. Recourse to displacement is imposed by more than one stimulus barrier. Freud identified the stimulus barrier of repression, but he neglected others.

The dream-censorship fashions symbols that function simultaneously as evasive distortions and moralizing revisions. No differently than the displacements, the moralizing revisions help qualify the dream for admission to consciousness. Freud was content to divide the ego's stimulus barriers into voluntary suppression and involuntary repression. He did not identify the particular stimulus barrier that the dream-work most frequently evades; and his oversight has since been perpetuated by psychoanalytic tradition. Most dream distortion functions, I suggest, to circumvent the commonplace stimulus barrier that is popularly termed "self-control." Self-control is an automatic but voluntarily reversible process of inhibition. Every child learns to control the needs to defecate and urinate, thirst, hunger, weeping and emotional distress, physical pain, and sexual arousal. When self-control has been achieved, the various primary processes are all routinely resisted whenever attention is devoted elsewhere. Should any of the desires become sufficiently intense, its conscious manifestation becomes irresistible. The production of self-control through the automatic activity of the stimulus barrier is proved by the frequent experience of completing an engrossing task before noticing a physical urge that is so intense that one assumes that it must have been building unnoticed for some time. Immediately after the task is done, one abruptly finds oneself hungry, thirsty, wounded, or in urgent need of elimination. The reversibility of self-control is most familiar in the case of sexual desire, whose conscious manifestation as an emotional and imaginative state may not occur until after a conscious decision has been made to allow oneself to become sexually aroused. Discovering oneself in a mood can follow the decision to do so, only because a stimulus barrier keeps the mood unconscious until the decision is made.

Like all of the ego's stimulus barriers (Rangell, 1974; 1976; 1980), self-control is also exercised in the moral sphere. Every child learns to restrict empathy to selected individuals on selected occasions. Most children and adolescents also learn more or less permanently to resist the demands of conscience for an ideal perfectionism, in deference to pragmatic considerations. These learned but automatic inhibitions are voluntarily reversible. It is generally possible to permit oneself to experience both empathy and demands for moral improvement. The stimulus barrier is also easily influenced in another manner. Moral standards are readily lowered through a type of self-control that institutionalizes falsehood. We speak of rationalization, self-deception, and hypocrisy when moral values are neither abandoned nor altered, but only excluded from consciousness by a stimulus barrier that systematically calls bad acceptable and right unnecessary. The knowledge of right and wrong is not abandoned, but subjected to displacement that misrepresents the moral values.

The learned, automatic, but voluntarily reversible stimulus barrier that constitutes self-control, in all its applications, is a preconscious ego function that bars both instinctual desires and conscience from consciousness. The distortions of dreams are concessions to the ego's stimulus barrier on the part of the superego.

Among the strengths of the prognostic function of the superego is its database. The superego is aware, as the ego's conscious decision-making function is not, of self-deceptions and inhibition-created ignorances that consciousness imposes by means of its stimulus barriers. Discrepancies between the conscious and inhibited portions of the ego are present to the superego not as conflicts but as logical contradictions or hypocrisies. In its role as arbiter of contradictions, the superego is invariably more knowledgeable than the ego. The superego is consequently able to arrive at valid solutions to many problems whose very existence is unrecognized by the ego's decision-making function. Again, the superego is not hampered in its reasoning, as is the ego's decision-making function, by the pleasurability of the conclusions attained. The superego has no internal stimulus barriers (Rangell, 1963). There is no division into unconscious and preconscious within the superego, and its reasoning processes are not subject to censorious inhibitions. The superego is able to pursue topics to their logical conclusions, regardless of whether they are pleasurable or painful. As well, the superego is not preoccupied, as is the ego's decision-making function, with the executive function of the psyche. It does not need to hurry to decisions in order to exercise voluntary control of the body and its real activities. The superego enjoys a luxury born of idleness to pursue single problems without distraction for extensive periods of time (Schilder & Kauders, 1926). Due to the breadth of the superego's database, its lack of internal stimulus barriers, and the extended time it can afford to devote to single problems, it is capable of significantly greater self-knowledge, wisdom, and intelligence than the ego, but only in specialized areas of performance.

Concluding Reflections

In reviewing dream theory, I have argued that Freud was wrong to restrict the dream-work to condensation, displacement, and considerations of representability. The fulfillments of wishes are not produced instantaneously and mechanically through condensation. On Freud's own showing, the superego definitely accomplishes a "secondary revision" or unconscious recasting of provisional wish-fulfillments in its capacity as a dream-censorship. The elaborations of punishment dreams are moral in content and themselves undergo symbolization. The conflicted fulfillments of wishes in anxiety dreams involve prognostic elaborations in time. The occurrence of words in dreams frequently attests to a rational linguistic competence on the part of the dream-work. Condensation is itself a rational process of metaphorization.

The superego's various contribution to dreams tend together to produce a prognostic assessment of the moral consequences of provisional wish-fulfillments. The superego's judgments are expressed by means of symbolization and reactive emotions that are included within the final content of the dreams. They are invariably latent when they are not also manifest. Due to the continuity of emotion from the latent to the manifest dream, at least part of the prognosis always manifests in undisguised form.

Due to the superego's contribution to dreams, every dream always has an ethical or existential message. This message proceeds at the emblematic level of dream interpretation. The existential contents of dreams should, in my opinion, be interpreted on a routine basis whenever dreams occur, as an integral component of daily life.

In clinical psychoanalysis, interpretation of dreams' existential concerns is an optimal means to address analysand's self-deceptions. To the extent that the elimination of hypocrisy mitigates the "secondary gains" of psychopathology, analytic work at the existential level is an irreplacible preparation for therapeutic work at the psychosexual level.

The emblematic interpretation of dreams also facilitates a therapeutic alliance with the superego. Had Freud helped Dora to understand the complexity of her dream's emblematic level of meaning, he would have enabled her to retain a sense of self-esteem—she remained a "good girl"—even as he broached the delicate topic of her ambivalent sexual feelings. He would have used her ethicality as an ally in his further exploration of her neurosis. He would have grounded her in the reality of her current relationships, even as he invited her to explore with him her fantasies of long ago. Instead of engaging Dora in a therapeutic alliance—in Winnicott's terms, a "holding space"—constructed out of her moral sensibility and real circumstances, Freud leapt immediately, disconnectedly, and shockingly to the topics of nocturnal urination and its unconsciously incestuous nature. When Freud interpreted, as incestuous, Dora's feelings for her father when, as a child, she had been taken by him to the toilet as a means to avoid bed-wetting, Freud may well have been right about the incestuous fantasies that continued to be at work in her neurosis. Nevertheless, in presenting his interpretation to her without exploring her dream's emblematic meaning and affirming both her moral integrity and contemporary circumstances, he left her without her normal points of reference—let me add, her healthy and realistic points of reference. Neglect of the therapeutic alliance with the superego is, in my opinion, an unnecessary hardship for clients during both the analysis and its termination.

Chapter 2

CONSCIENCE, EGO IDEALS, AND SELF-OBSERVATION

There are at least seven major formulations of superego theory—by Freud (1923a, p. 35), who hoped that it would explain "the higher, moral, supra-personal side of human nature"; by Alexander (1929), the first of many who treated the ego ideal and superego as separate agencies; by Klein (1929; 1932) and Jekels and Bergler (1934; 1940; Bergler, 1948; 1949; 1952; 1959), who tried in different ways to equate the superego with the death instinct; by Fairbairn (1943), who distinguished the superego from the internal saboteur; by Hartmann, Kris, and Loewenstein (1946), who limited the superego to unthinking responses learned by rote in childhood; and by Jacobson (1954b; 1964), who revived Nunberg's ([1932] 1955) view of the ego ideal and superego as developmental stages of a single psychic agency. These theories commonly credited the superego with the production of a guilty conscience, but otherwise often disagreed profoundly with each other.

Psychoanalysts' failure to develop a consensus regarding the superego may ultimately be traced to Freud's limited interest in the psychology of morality. He was content to quote F. T. Visher's remark, "What is moral is self-evident" (H. Hartmann, 1960, p. 14). He made no effort to develop a moral code on scientific principles, and traditional psychoanalytic theories remain incapable of doing so. Making a virtue out of necessity, psychoanalysts trumpet their scientific neutrality in avoiding moral pedagogy except in the cases of childhood neurosis and juvenile delinquency. However, an abdication of moral responsibility is never neutral. Psychoanalysis has its own ethic. Psychoanalysts display a relaxed attitude to human sexuality and show compassion for pathological behaviors that were formerly punished for moral turpitude. Their critique of the pathological features of traditional moralities (Menninger, 1973), taken together with their failure to provide a substitute, has contributed to the alarming proliferation of narcissism as a cultural norm (LaPiere, 1960; Wallach & Wallach, 1983). Erik Erikson (1958, p. 19) lamented: "We must grudgingly admit that even as we were trying to devise, with scientific determinism, a therapy for the few, we were led to promote an ethical disease among the many."

Psychoanalysts have repeatedly disputed the place of morality in their theories. In *The Interpretation of Dreams*, Freud (1900, pp. 207–8, 244) discussed a number of dreams whose unconscious wishes were repressed because their pleasure was infantile and morally objectionable. As an example, Freud offered the patricidal and incestuous wishes that are evoked in its audiences by the legend of King Oedipus.

> Here is one in whom these primaeval wishes of our childhood have been fulfilled, and we shrink back from him with the whole force of the repression by which those wishes have since that time been held down within us. . . . Like Oedipus, we live in ignorance of these wishes, repugnant to morality, which have been forced upon us by Nature (pp. 262–63).

Although Freud did not articulate the implicit generalization, his theory of the Oedipus complex eventually led Burrow (1914) to infer the logical corollary that "repression . . . is biologically a moral reaction" (p. 123). Burrow wrote:

> With the reaction of repression we are dealing with a reaction that is moral . . . at the heart of the neurosis the essential situation is a *moral revulsion*.
>
> This revulsion is directed unfailingly against the admission of primary, egoistic, organic, unconscious sexual trends. As we know, through psychoanalytic research, the different

neuroses represent but varying outcomes of a fundamental effort of evasion, but the stimulus to such evasion, being essentially a reaction against prohibition, is based in every instance upon a primary, biological intuition of *right and wrong* (p. 124).

As Fenichel (1928, p. 47) remarked, "Freud's doctrine of repression virtually implied that a sort of guilt-feeling acted as a criterion for the decisions of the repressing faculty." The implication that neuroses are symptoms of moral turpitude was unavoidable. Freud's topographic hypothesis, which divided the psyche into the rational and moral *Pcpt.-Cs.* and the irrational and symbolic *Ucs.*, permitted no other inference.

The idea that conscience is pathogenic was nevertheless completely unacceptable to Freud. The year after Burrow presented his conclusion at a psychoanalytic congress, Freud (1914) introduced his conception of the ego ideal. The theory implied that moral standards are personal ideals that vary with individuals and cultures. Freud excluded the possibility, inherent in his earlier work, that psychoanalytic criteria might furnish a single universal standard for morality. Ego ideals differ from person to person. An absolute moral code cannot be argued on biological grounds. Each person's ego maintains its own ideal standard of values. The pathogenesis of neurosis does not furnish evidence for the construction of a universal moral philosophy.

Freud nevertheless maintained what Pfister (1923) called the "optimistic view that the education to train the patient to be truthful to himself is a permanent protection against the danger of immorality" (p. 198). Erich Fromm (1947) commented that because "the pregenital orientations, characteristic of the dependent, greedy, and stingy attitudes, are ethically inferior to the genital, that is, productive, mature character . . . Freud's characterology . . . implies that virtue is the natural aim of man's development" (p. 45). Freud never resolved the inconsistency of his scientific value-neutrality with his normative personal morality and neither have psychoanalysts since.

Freud's (1923a) introduction of the structural model of the id, ego, and superego clarified the problem only in part. Although Freud separated the moral and medical issues by attributing morality to the superego and repression to the ego, he allowed that morality sometimes motivates the ego to exercise repression. At the same time, he warned that "there is a danger of over-estimating the part played in repression by the super-ego" (Freud, 1926, p. 94). Anna Freud ([1936] 1966) concluded that neurosis arises through an unreasonably demanding morality, whose "ideal standard, according to which sexuality is prohibited and aggression pronounced to be antisocial . . . is incompatible with psychic health" (p. 54). With this formulation, the theory of morality had come sufficiently free of the theory of neurosis that a morality might be pronounced either neurotic or wholesome, depending on whether it induced neurosis or not. Edward Bibring (1937) articulated the psychoanalytic consensus when he stated that the superego's "archaic severity must be reduced, its great tension in relation to the ego must be lessened, and it must in part be amalgamated with the ego. Its attitude of goodwill, its understanding and its kindly care must be increased; its functions must be better adapted to the ego's conditions of life and to reality" (p. 180).

Most psychoanalysts have since been content to distinguish healthy and neurotic moralities. The clinical perspective takes for granted the existence of morality as such, while limiting psychoanalysis to occasional explanations about preferences among different moral standards. The main issues remain unexplained. Psychoanalytic theory has no criteria for differentiating the moral and the immoral, nor for explaining how the human psyche can do so. Psychoanalysts regard morality as an integral part of human nature, but they take the view that the relativity of morality absolves them of responsibility to formulate theoretically what they take for granted in both their private lives and their professional conduct as clinicians—a code of moral values.

Ego Psychology's Denial of Conscience

Freud (1923a) intended superego theory as an explanation of conscience, but his contributions were not equal to the task. In *The Future of an Illusion* (1927), Freud described the superego as a residue of parental identifications that serves to internalize cultural values. In *Civilization and its Discontents* (1930), which nodded in Melanie Klein's direction, Freud described the superego as an internalization of aggression that directs aggression toward the ego. He suggested that the deflection of aggression away from the external world, to be employed as conscience in restraining further aggressiveness, produces the self-control that makes civilization possible (pp. 122–23). In *New Introductory Lectures on Psycho-Analysis* (1933), the superego and civilization had become so closely intertwined in Freud's thought that he described the superego as though it were self-perpetuating. Inculcated by parents in the child, the superego had similarly been instilled in them by their parents, and so has an integrity that is independent of the individuals who are the medium of its existence. "A child's super-ego is in fact constructed on the model not of its parents but of its parents' super-ego; the contents which fill it are the same and it becomes the vehicle of tradition and of all the time-resisting judgments of value which have propagated themselves in this manner from generation to generation" (p. 67).

Freud elaborated on the same point in his final summation of psychoanalytic theory, *An Outline of Psycho-Analysis* (1940). In this presentation, the superego *is* the psychic representative of culture.

The super-ego continues to play the part of an external world for the ego, although it has become a portion of the internal world. Throughout later life it represents the influence of a person's childhood, of the care and education given him by his parents and of his dependence on them—a childhood which is prolonged so greatly in human beings by a family life in common. And in all this it is not only the personal qualities of these parents that is making itself felt, but also everything that had a determining effect on them themselves, the tastes and standards of the social class in which they lived and the innate dispositions and traditions of the race from which they sprang . . . the super-ego . . . represents more than anything the cultural past, which a child has, as it were, to repeat as an after-experience during the few years of his early life (p. 206).

Freud explained the moral conservatism of religious traditions by postulating that a group superego maintains the same values across generations without significant reflection, change, or development. Although Freud's (1923a, p. 34) original description of the superego as "a precipitate in the ego" implied its performance of rational thought, his discussions of the superego's more or less direct replication, generation after generation, led many analysts to infer that the superego functions more or less by rote in applying the values it has acquired. In clinical discussions subsequent to Freud, the superego appears less as a thinking process than as a repository of cultural value judgments that is considerably refractory to learning (Furer, 1972). Psychoanalysis has not only declined to develop a psychology of morality. It has rationalized its position by denying, at a theoretic level, the very existence of personal moral responsibility.

The American school of psychoanalytic ego psychology has been particularly negligent in this regard. Hartmann, Kris, and Loewenstein (1946, p. 30) attributed moral reasoning exclusively to the ego and reduced the superego from the psychical agency responsible for ideals, conscience, self-observation, humor, and dream distortion, to an agency limited to rote repetitions of acquired value judgments. The enlargement of ego psychology's concept of the ego at the expense of the superego limited the superego to a set of borrowed values. It was a structure but not a process.

Ego psychology's reduction of conscience to a collection of unreasoning prejudices that have been acquired by rote, followed as a corollary of the concept of psychic structures. In the "topographical hypothesis" of *The Interpretation of Dreams*, Freud (1900) suggested that there are two categorically different *processes* of thinking, one unconscious and instinctual, and the other conscious and rational. He termed them the "primary" and "secondary processes," respectively (p. 598). Both processes were assumed to be innate neurophysiological endowments. In *The Ego and the Id*, Freud (1923a) advanced what has since come to be called the "structural hypothesis," in which he renamed the primary and secondary processes, respectively, as the id and the ego.

The change in the processes' names coincided with Freud's introduction of the notion of psychic *structure*. As Freud used the term, structures are invariably acquired, learned, and developed. In the structural hypothesis, Freud (1923a) derived the ego from the id. "The ego is not sharply separated from the id; its lower portion merges into it" (p. 24). Indeed, "the ego is that part of the id which has been modified by the direct influence of the external world" (p. 25). As for the superego, it was similarly not an inherently discrete entity. It was "a grade in the ego, a differentiation within the ego" (p. 28).

Freud never acknowledged, much less resolved, the inconsistency of identifying the primary process with the id and the secondary process with the ego, when the primary and secondary processes were inborn, while the id, ego, and superego were developmentally acquired. Neither have later psychoanalysts addressed the issues satisfactorily. Most analysts have simply ignored the problem. However, H. Hartmann (1939) argued persuasively that the ego possesses a primary autonomy that is inborn. Hartmann, Kris, and Loewenstein (1946) later codified this position for American ego psychology as an explicit correction of Freud's structural model.

> Freud speaks of a gradual differentiation of the ego from the id.... Freud's formulation ... implies that the infant's equipment existing at birth is part of the id. It seems however that the innate apparatus and reflexes cannot all be part of the id (pp. 35–36).

Few psychoanalysts, with the notable exceptions of G. Klein (1962) and Loewald (1980), have ever attempted to maintain the exclusively structural character of Freud's structural hypothesis. Hartmann's emphasis of autonomous, inborn ego functions reinstated the inborn status of the primary and secondary processes— the id and the ego. However, he and his co-workers explicitly denied that the superego has any hard-wired, innate features. "There is no specific apparatus whose maturation is essential for the growth of conscience; only a certain stage of development of intellectual life forms an essential precondition ... the formation of the superego is the result of social influences and of processes of identification" (Hartmann, Kris, & Loewenstein, 1946, p. 48).

Ego psychology's denial that conscience reasons is a logical corollary of Hartmann's position. If the superego is a structure, it cannot be a process that thinks, reasons, deliberates, or judges. It can be no more than a body of data to which the ego refers while performing its own ("secondary") process thinking.

Although ego psychology's model of the superego dominates psychoanalytic thought in North America today, it was argued from theory and not from data. It is an arbitrary, axiomatic stipulation; and it is unable to account for the variety of conscience. Erich Fromm (1947) accurately characterized the conventional rote theory of the superego as an account of authoritarian conscience alone.

Anything can become the content of conscience if only it happens to be part of the system of commands and prohibitions embodied in the father's Super-Ego and the cultural tradition. *Conscience in this view is nothing but internalized authority.* Freud's analysis of the Super-Ego is the analysis of the "authoritarian conscience" only (p. 43).

Fromm maintained that Freud had failed to discuss "humanistic ethics" that have their basis in "the principle that only man himself can determine the criterion for virtue and sin, and not an authority transcending him" (p. 22).

In an independent critique, Sagan (1988) emphasized that "the superego is essentially amoral and can be as easily immoral as moral. Within a slave society, the superego legitimates slavery. Within a racist or sexist society, the superego demands racism and sexism. And in a Nazi society, the superego commands one to live up to genocidal ideals" (p. 9). "The superego is not just the internal representative of the parents' moral values but of *all their values,* good and bad, moral and immoral" (p. 19).

Observing that "there is a moral system within the psyche *independent* of the value system of the culture" (p. 23), Sagan maintained that there is "an instrument in the psyche that can differentiate the moral and immoral attributes of the superego" (p. 14). He identified this "instrument" with conscience.

Conscience, unlike the superego, knows clearly which actions are moral and which immoral . . . conscience, unlike the superego, is incapable of corruption and pathology. It may be silenced or paralyzed, but one can never accurately speak of a diseased conscience (p. 14).

Sagan's choice of terminology is not helpful, but his argument is apt. People regularly criticize cultural values on the basis of private moral standards. The personal morality cannot plausibly be ascribed to the ego because it is often experienced as ego-alien inspiration or obligation, and it is not felt to be a product of the self's own voluntary reasoning. Sagan erred, however, in treating conscience and the superego as mutually exclusive mental functions. The unthinking superego of American ego psychology is a caricature. It is not an accurate account of something other than conscience. It is plainly and simply an incompetent formulation. It does not correspond to reality.

Let us approach the problem from another direction. A few psychoanalytic writers have elected a theoretic option that ego psychology has neglected. Lichtenstein (in Goodman, 1965) postulated "the decisive, though not exclusive, role of an inherent factor, not derivable from trans-valued outside demands, in the formation and function of the superego." He offered:

> three main reasons why it is difficult to trace the sense of urgent "oughtness" to internalized outside demands: first, the logical *non sequitur* existing between the proposition of identification with parental demands and the development of self-imposed moral rules; second, the fact that historically great moral decisions seem typically to dispense with the very outside demands that the individual had at one time accepted without questioning; third, the problem of the individual selectivity of identifications (p. 177).

Rubinfine (1959), Schur (in Rubinfine, 1959), and Jacobson (1964, p. 93) similarly suggested that the superego has innate or inherent factors that contribute to the autonomy of conscience from both infantile traumata and the opinions of other people.

Another proof that the superego has its basis in an innate, autonomous factor is the striking convergence of moral systems cross-culturally. What needs explanation is not the divergence of different moral systems, but the fact that they show any resemblances at all. Summarizing anthropologists' findings, H. Hartmann (1960) asserted:

> According to Kluckhohn, murder, unlimited lying and stealing are everywhere valued negatively; also something like a principle of "reciprocity" is recognized everywhere. Montagu states

that murder is generally considered a crime; some incest regulations are universal; nowhere is cannibalism regular practice. Also, the duty of the adults to take care of the children is generally accepted; a certain respect for private property is, too, and so is respect for the dead of one's own group (p. 83).

Hartmann noted but was unable to account for these ethical convergencies.

Ticho (1972) inferred that moral universals must be based in an innate and unvarying aspect of the human psyche. "The values of a mature, autonomous superego may be different from society to society, but it is surprising how similar are the ideals of many religions, whatever the ritual or the credo: e.g., overcoming self-centeredness and a concern for other human beings are universal goals, and as such can be seen as of universal autonomous superego content" (p. 221).

What I shall argue is that conscience is not a structure but a process. It is a particular application of a more general process that deserves recognition as a "tertiary process" alongside the ego and the id.

Conscience as a Wish-Fulfillment

Let us begin with an analysis of conscience. Conscience may manifest as a judgment of value after the fact of an action. Conscious experience of retrospective judgments of conscience may consist of the judgment of value alone.

From the last quarter of the first year of life, conscience may instead manifest before the fact as a prognostic judgment on a potential future action. "Moral emotions ... are anticipatory; that is, they are 'signal affects'. They portend or represent in some way the consequences of an intended outcome" (Emde, 1988, p. 35). When conscience is anticipatory, its manifest experience always entails at least two mental elements: (1) an intention, desire, or perceived opportunity, that is followed by (2) a reactive evaluation whose expression may be emotional and/or cognitive in form. Intermediate steps that link the initial intention with the concluding evaluation may or may not be present to consciousness. The evaluation may seem to manifest to the conscious self as though coming from outside it. It may come as something of a surprise, with the autonomy, integrity, and self-completion of an inspiration, intuition, or revelation.

Whenever conscience is anticipatory, it exhibits the structure of a wish-fulfillment. It begins with a wish regarding a future action. The wish is entertained not as an idle fantasy but with the seriousness of purpose of an intention. In cases when the intention is unconscious, it is consciously experienced as a manifest opportunity. We may hypothesize that in all events, the intention is unconsciously assimilated to the knowledge of a similar intention that was implemented in the past. Knowledge of the consequences of past actions may have been acquired through personal experience, through observation of another person's experience, through hearsay, or by precept. However the knowledge may be acquired, the past sequence is condensed with the present intention and projected into the future as its implementation. The imagined implementation is adjusted more or less realistically to future circumstances. Once the initial desire has been developed unconsciously into an imagined future scenario, the latter is evaluated reactively from a moral perspective.

To summarize: the anticipatory function of conscience has four features: (i) a present intention; (2) its condensation with a similar wish that was fulfilled in the past; (3) a reasoning process that develops the condensation into an imagination that conforms more closely with future realities; and (4) a judgment of value concerning the present intention.

Whether conscience is retrospective and limited to judgments of value, or anticipatory and additionally imaginative of future scenerios, it exhibits the same variety of mental functions that is discernible in dreams. In both dreams and conscience, wishes are developed into possible future scenarios that are made the basis of reactive judgments of value. Moral imagination is speculative and may be inaccurate, but it is neither a flight from nor a substitution for reality. Hanna Segal (1991) characterized this distinction as the difference between the "what-if" of imagination and the "as-if" of fantasy. "This kind of imagination does not deny reality to produce an 'as-if' world, but explores possibilities" (p. 107).

Although the historical sequence of psychoanalytic discoveries has led me to discuss dreams prior to conscience, it would be more appropriate for purposes of theory to reverse the priority. Dreams may be described as forms that conscience takes when it manifests to a sleeping ego. The significant differences between waking conscience and dreams regularly owe to the variables of sleep. Because the ego must concern itself with reality during wakefulness, the ego's activities are the major source of the wishes that conscience addresses during waking consciousness. Dreams are often fantastic because the wishes that are permitted to occupy the mind during sleep exhibit a wider variety of concerns. The concerns include trivialities for which consciousness has no time, as well as repressions. Because the involuntary stimulus barriers of the ego do not relax during sleep, dreams compensate for their wishes' versatility by taking increased recourse to distortion through condensations and displacements.

To summarize: A judgment of conscience that pertains to a past event consists of a reactive moral evaluation. A judgment of conscience that anticipates a possible future event begins with a wish-fulfilling imagination of the future scenario, to which a reactive moral evaluation is attached. Much of the imagination may remain unconscious or preconscious; the reactive evaluation is regularly conscious.

When conscience is inhibited, its latent content remains conscience, but its manifest content undergoes symbolization in order to evade the stimulus barrier(s). The result during sleep is a transformation of conscience into the dream.

The Reactive Evaluation

How does the superego come by its reactive evaluations? Some of its values it borrows from other people, but in other cases it is able to formulate moral decisions on its own. It does so, I suggest, on the basis of empathy.

The German word *Einfühlung*, literally "feeling together with," was devised by Theodor Lipps in 1897 in reference to the esthetic experience of art. Lipps's term was translated into English as "empathy," perhaps first by Vernon Lee in 1904. Subsequent usage applied Lipps's concept in both esthetic and interpersonal contexts (Deutsch & Madle, 1975; Post, 1980).

In his psychoanalytic writings, Freud (1921) used the term *Einfühlung* only once. In his view, empathy is "the mechanism by means of which we are enabled to take up any attitude at all towards another mental life" (p. 110, n. 2). Freud (1915c) explained his concept of a *conditio sine qua non* for the perception of other psyches in a passage where, however, he happened not to use the term "empathy."

Consciousness makes each of us aware only of his own states of mind; that other people, too, possess a consciousness is an inference which we draw by analogy from their observable utterances and actions, in order to make this behaviour of theirs intelligible to us. (It would no doubt be psychologically more correct to put it in this way: that without any special reflection we attribute to everyone else our own constitution and therefore our consciousness as well, and that this identification is a *sine qua non* of our understanding.) ... the assumption of a consciousness in them rests upon an inference and cannot share the immediate certainly which we have of our own consciousness (p. 168).

Freud here characterized empathy as an inference regarding other people's experience that is drawn by analogy from one's own experience. It is, in short, an act of imagination. Buie (1981, p. 283) emphasized that empathy depends on "ordinary sensory perception." "The relevant perceptual cues from the patient must be assembled as a sort of *ad hoc* model ... which is descriptive and not affective, [but] can then be used ... as a basis for creative imitation ... of a corresponding affective-impulsive-ideational state" (p. 297).

Basch (1983) and Nathanson (1986) argued that the interpersonal perceptions in empathy are limited to physiological *affects*, which are expressed in facial features, body posture, and so forth. The assembly of the perceptions into conscious experiences of *emotions* are reconstructions. Due to the discrepancy between perceived affects and imagined feelings, empathy is regularly inaccurate. "We never really share the other person's emotion because each of us has lived too complex a life, has formed associations to these innate affects based on experiences which are different despite their general similarity. Your experience of shame is not mine, your anger is not my anger. Yet through empathy I may clench my jaw when you feel angry, and look away in embarrassment when you are shamed" (Nathanson, 1986, p. 175).

Olden (1953) noted that empathy may also disclose more than another person's conscious emotions. Empathy "has the capacity *ad libitum* to trespass the object's screens of defenses, behind which the real feelings may hide, as in the case of the child who clowns, the child who clings, etc." (p. 115). Greenson (1967) remarked that in empathizing with the feelings of another, "one partakes of the quality of the feelings and not the quantity." Beres (1968) emphasized that "there is no loss of capacity to distinguish between self-representation and object-representation. . . . Empathy may enter into the feelings of sympathy or pity, but is not identical to these" (pp. 364–65).

Empathy is accomplished at different speeds by different people. Kohut (1981a) remarked that empathy "may, occasionally, be used seemingly intuitively by experts: that is, via high-speed mental processes of observation that identify complex configurations preconsciously and at great speed. But mostly . . . empathy is used nonintuitively, ploddingly, if you wish, by trial and error" (p. 540). Greenson (1967) noted that empathy "can be consciously instigated or interrupted; and it can occur silently and automatically, oscillating with other forms of relating to people" (pp. 368–69).

Although it has sometimes been suggested that empathy may manifest in various forms (Olinick, 1969, p. 43), empathy is characterized by a distinctly emotional way of seemingly knowing another person's inner experience. The emotional aspect of empathy may manifest wordlessly on its own. It may manifest together with verbal ideas that elaborate its content. It may be attended by concrete images or elaborated fantasies. For definitional purposes, however, neither verbal ideas nor fantasies qualify as empathy in the absence of the distinctive experience of seemingly sharing a knowledge of emotion in an emotional manner (Stotland, Mathews, Sherman, Hansson, & Richardson, 1978, pp. 14–15).

Empathy has no necessarily benevolent, moral, or prosocial bias. Kohut (1981b) emphasized that empathy does not imply compassion or affection, but may be utilized in the service of malevolence. "If you want to hurt somebody, and you want to know where his vulnerable spot is, you have to know him before you can put in the right dig. . . . When the Nazis attached sirens to their dive bombers, they knew with fiendish empathy how people on the ground would react to that with destructive anxiety. This was correct empathy, but not for friendly purposes" (p. 529). Empathy can also be antipathetic of hostile people. "Empathic understanding of the demagogue or the false friend . . . far from leading to love or attraction, can give rise to hatred, anger, revulsion, and the urge to distance oneself rather than to get closer" (Basch, 1983, p. 122).

Although "the subjective experience of empathy is one of direct, non-mediated knowing" that is attended by a "feeling of certainty" (Olinick, 1969, p. 12), the feeling is an illusion. Like the empathic response to a work of art, the empathic experience of seemingly or apparently feeling or knowing emotionally what another person feels is necessarily and inherently an exercise of imagination (E. Balint, 1993). Empathy is at best "approximate or roughly congruent" because it "is based to a great extent on remembered, corresponding affective states of one's own" (Schafer, 1959, p. 347). For the same reason, "the reliability of empathy declines, the more dissimilar the observed is from the observer" (Kohut, 1959, p. 214). Kohut (1981a, p. 540) added that empathic "misperception occurs either because we are guided by erroneous expectations, by misleading theories that distort our perception . . . or because we are not sufficiently conscientious and rigorous in immersing ourselves for protracted periods in the field of our observation."

The capacity for empathy varies from person to person and occasion to occasion (Ferreira, 1961, p. 95). Its accuracy tends to increase with cognitive and emotional developmental. "As a child begins to read another's facial expressions and body attitudes, he must bring them into coordination with his own growing repertoire of emotional states in order for empathy to emerge" (Shapiro, 1974, p. 18). The practice of empathy tends, however, to decrease with age.

Mostly subserved by somesthetic and olfactory sensations in the first few months of life, and later mainly by visual and auditory (the "third ear") ones, empathy gradually seems to taper off and decrease through the years, "inhibited and overlaid" by the development of the secondary thought processes, to become in the adult a relatively infrequent manifestation (Ferreira, 1961, p. 95).

Sawyier (1975) suggested that the gradual loss of empathy with aging may be due to the development of a stimulus barrier. "If it makes sense to claim that the feelings of people (and probably of other animals) around us are themselves a kind of input, that I am subject to them, as it were, then it may make good sense to extend the concept of stimulus-barrier to include emotional inputs" (pp. 42–43). A child's autonomy may require a desensitization or inhibition of empathy. On the other hand, Ferreira (1961) emphasized that empathy in adults has a wholesome diagnostic significance. "In the adult, empathy must . . . be seen as a phenomenon that characterizes the healthy individual, as a manifestation of a function that could have survived only in a relatively normally developed ego" (pp. 99–100).

Loewald (1979, p. 403) asserted that "empathy . . . play[s] a significant part in everyday interpersonal relations"; and French and Erika Fromm (1964) described the practical problem-solving of the dream as empathic thinking. In their view, empathic thinking differs from reality-testing and logic, but underlies rational behavior (pp. 86-87).

By "empathic understanding," we mean understanding another person's feelings and behavior by identifying with him, by imagining ourselves in his situation and motivated to act as he does. In order to perform this imaginative act of identification . . . we supplement our observation of the other person with knowledge of how we might behave under similar circumstances (pp. 138–40).

French and Fromm (1964, pp. 150–55) equated empathic thinking with the role-giving, role-taking, and analogical thinking discussed in social role theory (Sarbin, 1950). Although empathy has an emotional dimension that is not always present in role-taking, it may be appropriate to think of empathy as a particular vicissitude of a general psychic process that thinks in terms of self-and-object relationships. Thinking about other people is a manifest content of most dreams; 85 percent of the dreams of normal adults depict persons other than the dreamer (Ephron & Carrington, 1967, pp. 86–87). Empathic thinking, in all its forms, may be considered a type of thinking that invariably considers both self and other.

Furer (1967) argued that empathy is responsible for the origin of guilt in the child. In cases of the empathic "experience [of] the painful quality of an affect in the other person that . . . [has] been evoked in the observed person by an act of the observer," it some-times happens that "either the child ends up saying, 'I am sorry,' in actual words, or else this is to be understood from the nature of his consoling behaviour toward the object" (p. 277). "It is the ego's increasing capacity to sustain memory, to maintain the love of the object in the face of frustration, and to empathize, that results in the affects of remorse and later in guilt" (p. 279). What Furer observed was indeed empathy: a transmuting of sympathetic hurt, through self-observation, into a knowledge of having caused hurt. Due to the child's love, the knowledge of responsibility led to sorrow, guilt, remorse, and reparation. Should the knowledge of responsibility instead coincide with hostility for the object, the empathic recognition of the object's hurt might lead to self-satisfaction and continued aggression. Because empathy is not tied to the object's feelings as sympathy is, it leads as easily to "identification with the aggressor" (A. Freud, [1936] 1966) as to "identification with the comforter" (Furer, 1967).

Theoretic accounts of empathy have been various. A series of writers have written of "transient," "partial," or "temporary identification" (Fenichel 1945, p. 511; Weiss, 1952, p. 60; Furer, 1967, p. 277; Greenson, 1960, p. 423; 1967, p. 369; Beres & Arlow, 1974, p. 33; Solnit, 1982, pp. 207–8). These formulations are inconsistent, however, with the distinction between self and object that is maintained throughout the experience of empathy. Equally unacceptable, and for the same reason, are the several formulations that postulate "merging," "intrapsychic fusion of self-image and object image," "a loosening or even suspension of the subject-object split," "nondifferentiation," or "letting go of ego boundaries" (Schafer, 1968, p. 153; Olinick, 1969, p. 43; Loewald, 1970, p. 284; Shapiro, 1974; Eyre, 1978, p. 354).

More nuanced formulations have attempted to comprehend empathy by resolving it into two processes. Fenichel (1945) articulated this theoretic option by speaking of "two acts: (a) an identification with the other person, and (b) an awareness of one's own feelings after the identification, and in this way an awareness of the object's feelings" (p. 511; see also Fliess, 1942, p. 214; Olden, 1953, p. 113; Kohut, 1959, 1977; French & Fromm, 1964, pp. 145–49; Post, 1980, pp. 278–79). I have elsewhere argued, however, that unitive thinking is a category of cognition—comparable to time perception, mathematical reasoning, and so forth—with its own developmental line (Merkur, 1999). The schema that produces identification, with its loss of the subject-object distinction, is less realistic than empathy. In Piagetian terms, identification exhibits an *assimilation* of reality to unitive ideas, where empathy shows greater *accommodation* of unitive ideas to reality. Feelings are projected in empathy, but the contents of empathic imaginations conform with the demand of reality that the feelings be acknowledged, both unconsciously and consciously, as feelings that belong to another (Margulies, 1989, p. 88). Empathy may nevertheless be resolved into two components: (1) an *imaginative construction* of the subjective feelings of another person, (2) that is joined together with *introspection* concerning one's own feelings in response.

The process of empathy conforms with the general pattern of wish-fulfillment with one exception. Empathic imagination is speculative and may be inaccurate, but it is neither a flight from reality nor a substitution for it. The empathic process begins with the establishment of a wish to know what another person is feeling. The wish concerns the emotions implied by sense perceptions and other knowledge of the other person. It is because the motivating desire pertains to cognitive materials that the latter are utilized in the unconscious incubation of empathic thinking. The wish to know is unconsciously developed into an imagined knowledge, *ex hypothesi* through its condensation with a past instance in which the knowledge was available. In empathic thinking, the past experience of knowing the emotional significance of particular facial expressions, bodily posture, and so forth, is often the past experience of the subject. However, it may also be based on past experiences of other people, people's statements regarding their feelings, and so forth. Following the condensation that produces it, the imagined feeling becomes the topic of a reactive evaluation. The evaluation presupposes the distinction between the self and the other person, and it formulates feelings introspectively that react or respond to the feelings attributed to the other person.

Empathy is the reasoning process of conscience, but conscience is not co-extensive with empathy. Empathy accomplishes more than conscience alone. "Standards for personal appearance, vocational prestige and social status, matters of etiquette, questions of artistic excellence and beauty, can all fall under the sway of the superego" (Wallwork, 1991, p. 223). Empathy is not limited to the context of interpersonal relations. In the original esthetic context of the term, empathy consists of an imagining of the feelings implied by a work of art. Esthetic appreciation unconsciously imagines the feelings that moved the artist to create the artwork; it also includes a reactive or evaluative component that manifests the feelings that one would oneself have to have had if one were the artist.

When empathic imagination addresses the circumstances of how another person does or will feel in response to one's actions, and the attitude to the other person is loving rather than antipathetic, the reactive emotion is invariably a moral judgment. In empathy, one imagines another person feeling X, and one appreciates that, in that event, one would oneself feel Y. Conscience adds further details. Retroactive judgments of conscience proceed on the basis that event A has caused another person to feel X, leading oneself to feel Y. Anticipatory judgments imagine that the future eventuality of A, leading the other person to feel X, and oneself to react with Y. In either event, one feels self-esteem that one has been or will be responsible for the feeling that another person has been or will be made to feel, or else one evaluates one's own responsibility with guilt and regret.

Neurotic Guilt

The distinction between conscience and neurotic guilt is readily demonstrated through the analysis of a reaction-formation. A reaction-formation is ordinarily understood as a "psychological attitude or habitus diametrically opposed to a repressed wish, and constituted as a reaction against it (e.g., bashfulness countering exhibitionistic tendencies)" (Laplanche & Pontalis, 1973, p. 376). Classical examples of reaction-formations include "an exaggerated prudery or purity as a defence against sexual interests, an exaggerated brusqueness or petty aggressiveness as a defence against shyness or inferiority feelings . . . an exaggerated defence or humility (à la Uriah Heep) to cover a crude and avaricious egoism . . . a quasi-obsessive kindliness, friendliness, or humanity overlying aggressiveness, and an excessive concern about some other person's health or welfare to hide unconscious hostility and death wishes against that person" (Flugel, 1945, pp. 69–70). Because reaction-formations are always instances of self-deception or hypocrisy, and because the conscious values that they impose are excessive rather than wholesome (Flugel, 1945, p. 70), the superego's involvement in reaction-formation has contributed to psychoanalysts' generally negative view of the superego.

The notion of diametrical opposition between the unconscious and the conscious portions of a reaction-formation goes back to the topographic hypothesis. Freud (1915b) stated:

> At first the repression is completely successful; the ideational content is rejected and the affect is made to disappear. As a substitutive formation there arises an alteration in the ego . . . by intensifying an opposite . . . the vanished affect comes back in its transformed shape . . . the rejected idea is replaced by a *substitute by displacement* (p. 157).

Working with the topographic hypothesis, it would be possible, for example, to see a reaction-formation in the belief that viciously cruel punishment is a healthy discipline that does a child good. As with all "moral indignation which permits envy or hate to be acted out under the guise of virtue" (Fromm, 1947, p. 236), the cruelty is unconscious and the self-righteousness is conscious.

The tripartite model of the psyche significantly altered the analysis of reaction-formations. It introduced the idea that the unconscious portion of a reaction-formation is not repressed as a response to helplessness. It is instead maintained in a continual state of suppression because it is objectionable to the superego. Freud (1926) wrote: "The exaggerated degree and compulsive character of the affection alone betray the fact that it is not the only one present but is continually on the alert to keep the opposite feeling under suppression, and enable us to postulate the operation of a process which we call repression by means of *reaction-formation* (in the ego)" (p. 102). For example, self-righteousness masking cruelty is not evidence of a harsh or severe conscience. Neither the self-righteousness nor the cruelty are judgments of conscience. What conscience contributes is guilt in response to the cruelty. The ego maintains its denial of the guilt through continual suppression; fantasies of self-righteousness arise subsequently as symptomatic compromise formations.

A further addition to the theory of reaction-formations was contributed by Bergler (1948), who initially suggested that reaction-formations invariably have more complicated, three-layer structures.

> The original wish never comes to the surface directly. *An Id wish is presented (Layer 1). The Super Ego protests and a defense mechanism is created (Layer 2).* The Super Ego protests, however, even against the defense, and *a second defense mechanism is established (Layer 3).* This second defense mechanism is the neurotic symptom (p. 16).

In later presentations, Bergler (1959) rephrased the same theory as a five-layer model. The only substantive change between the two presentations was a linkage of reaction-formation to masochism—a speculation that I am not prepared to endorse.

Bergler's three-layer model suffices for present purposes. Let us take the example of a woman with an unresolved parental conflict whose content is repressed and unconscious (Bergler's Layer 1). One symptom of the conflict is a general attitude of jealousy that is displaced from the parent to people quite generally. Because conscience finds indiscriminate jealousy to be morally objectionable, the individual avoids awareness of her guilt not by abandoning her jealousy, but by avoiding consciousness of her jealousy (Layer 2). What occupies her consciousness is a practice of fault-finding. Whenever faults can be found in others, there is no logical reason to be jealous of them. Through fault-finding, consciousness is avoided of both jealousy and its moral disapproval by conscience. However, because the fault-finding is unjustified, it too is found morally objectionable by conscience. The individual then deflects consciousness of guilt a second time, for example, by indulging in self-deceiving fantasies that rationalize her hostility as objectively valid criticism (Layer 3).

In this instance, as in all cases of reaction-formations, there is nothing intrinsically or inherently unconscious about the feelings or behavior in Layer 2. Indeed, it is precisely because those feelings or behavior are not repressed and will manifest consciously if they are allowed to do so that symptomatic compromise formations result in the fault-finding of Layer 3. Because Layer 2 could be conscious but happens not to be, it is technically described as *suppressed and preconscious*, rather than repressed and unconscious. In most cases, however, the suppression is maintained only imperfectly, and consciousness of Layer 2 occurs from time to time. Aspects of Layer 2 also typically manifest together with Layer 3 in an ambivalent or conflicted symptom. What alone is truly unconscious is the traumatic childhood experience(s) of Layer 1, whose symptoms constitutes Layer 2.

Where does the superego fit in this process? Because the moral disapproval of Layer 2 motivates the development of Layer 3, psychoanalysts working with Freud's two-layer model have assumed that the reaction in Layer 3 meets the approval of conscience. A considerable literature naively regards the exaggerated or excessive sentiments and behavior in Layer 3 as evidence of the superego's excessive demands. Bergler (1949) claimed instead that the reaction in Layer 3 is evaluated by the conscience as the lesser of two evils. The superego's own value structure is not disclosed by the neurotic excesses of the demands. "Every neurotic operates intrapsychically on the basis of acceptance of guilt for the lesser crime" (p. 97).

The incorrect assumption that the neurotic values that form the "lesser crime" in Layer 3 are the actual values of conscience has kept analysts from recognizing reaction-formations in the many cases in which the conscious materials of Layer 3 are more morally reprehensible than the preconscious ones of Layer 2. For example, a reaction-formation is described in the joke, "I don't know why he hates me; I never did him any favors." Here an inability to tolerate feelings of gratitude is understood to result in hatred of the benefactor. The suppressed gratitude is presumably neurotic in character; it may, for example, be criticized by the superego for its undue obsequiousness. Psychoanalytic literature does not refer to this commonplace of narcissistic disorders as a reaction-formation, but it is one nevertheless. It inverts the commonly remarked pattern of impiety being suppressed through excessive piety. It instead suppresses excessive piety (Layer 2) by manifesting unjustified aggression (Layer 3).

Another reaction-formation whose third layer is more morally reprehensible than its second is the practice of blaming the victim. Blaming the victim proceeds on the fallacious logic that two wrongs make oneself right. Wrongdoing is rationalized as fair treatment when an equal or worse failing is imputed to one's victim. Whenever blame is projected to rationalize aggression, a knowledge of innocence is being avoided. As always, Layer 1 of the reaction-formation remains unconscious and almost certainly involves a significant person in childhood, rather than the victim of the current aggression.

Flights from conscience may not logically be equated with conscience itself. However, the methodological goal of economy in theory led Freud to treat the instincts together with the repressed under the term "id," and both perception-consciousness and the self-representation under the term "ego." An equivalent methodological oversimplification also skewed his model of the superego. Healthy and neurotic guilt are not wholesome and morbid activities of a single psychic agency, but the products of separate agencies. The superego can be savage as well as civilized; it governs conduct in both war and peace. However, the masochism and the sadism of neurotic guilt are not superego phenomena. They are instead to be counted among the so-called defenses of the ego. Fairbairn (1943) described them collectively as the "anti-libidinal subject" or "internal saboteur." As Winnicott (1960a, p. 470) noted, "It is in health only that the classical superego . . . can be observed."

Value Testing

Conscience may borrow values, but in health it does not do so uncritically. Value formation is a superego function. Because the superego is able to invent its own values, it is also able to test the values that it borrows. Sometimes it confirms, sometimes it modifies, and sometimes it opposes the values that example and precept have taught.

The empathic imagination by which conscience formulates its values is also regularly used to test existing values. By developing empathic judgments concerning both real and hypothetical situations, conscience is enabled to decide whether ostensible values are truly valuable. Value testing is presumably an ongoing process during both wakefulness and sleep that is often barred from consciousness during wakefulness. As a result, value testing is particularly prominent as a function of dreams. Dora's dream, for example, evaluated the moral complexity of her feelings and behavior in response to Mr. K. Because the latent emotional content of dreams succeeds in manifesting even when the cognitive content is displaced, Dora's value testing was able to manifest through her dreams, despite her conscious resistance to the attendant cognitions.

Serota (1976) suggested that value testing should be considered an integral component of psychoanalysts' work with their analysands.

The analyst must separate the patient's imperatives and ideals and the structure of his moral codes, and the problems of confronting his attitudes with the codes of his family and more generally of the culture within which he lives, from the personal moral valuations of himself and the material presented in analysis. Thus the analyst's value system is as much a 'given' as is his intellect, interests and so on. Thus, also, *value testing* is as much a part of the therapeutic process as is *reality testing* (p. 373).

It is not a question of psychoanalysts' imposing their own values on their clients, but of facilitating their clients' testing of the values that they present in analysis (p. 375; see also Nicholas, 1994).

Langs (1994a, pp. 43–58; 1994c, pp. 21–24) independently remarked on the unconscious self-observation, empathy, and so forth, by which an analysand validates the progress of a psychoanalysis. Langs urged psychoanalysts to attend carefully to the client's unconscious validation and rely on it as more truthful and self-knowing than the client's conscious validation.

Through its value-testing function, conscience may take up a value of any origin, learned or self-devised. After testing the value's application to different situations, conscience may install the value as a more or less permanent component of its value system. The moral insight must then be worked through, in order to become integrated within the total personality.

The Dependency of Conscience

Not only do judgments of conscience consist of self-evaluations in response to interpersonal behavior, but moral standards are themselves dependent, in varying degrees, on interpersonal relations throughout life. Children begin by adopting and value testing the moral standards of their love objects before they develop a general moral code at the onset of latency. However, Waelder (1937) remarked that the adoption of new values continues "probably till the end of the twenties" (p. 438; cf. Greenson, 1954, p. 211). Sterba (1934) went further. He contended that the therapeutic action of psychoanalysis has its parallel in superego formation. Where superego formation consists of "the powerful establishment of moral demands," psychoanalysis makes "a demand for a revised attitude appropriate to the adult personality" (p. 12). Insofar as psychoanalysis brings repressed materials to consciousness, it resolves fixations and makes previously inaccessible materials available for sublimation into superego content. Wholly new materials are also learned directly through the patient's identification with the psychoanalyst (Bibring, 1937; Glover, 1937; Strachey, 1937; Novey, 1958; Parens, 1970).

Moral standards are similarly mutable when falling in love. With the commencement of a romantic involvement, the opinions of the beloved contribute to a profound modification of the superego for the duration of the love. Indeed, psychoanalytic theory implicates the superego in the phenomenon of romantic love. Discussing the experience of "being in love," Freud (1921) noted the proximity of the beloved and the ego ideal—a term that he was then temporarily using to designate the agency that he later named the superego.

Contemporaneously with this 'devotion' of the ego to the object, which is no longer to be distinguished from a sublimated devotion to an abstract idea, the functions allotted to the ego ideal entirely cease to operate. The criticism exercised by that agency is silent; everything that the object does and asks for is right and blameless. Conscience has no application to anything that is done for the sake of the object; in the blindness of love remorselessness is carried to the pitch of crime. The whole situation can be completely summarized in a formula: *The object has been put in the place of the ego ideal* (p. 113; Freud's emphasis).

Chasseguet-Smirgel (1976; 1985) suggested that the ego ideal is projected onto the beloved because a person's love for the beloved is a projection of the ego's love for the ego ideal. "In the state of love—from the outset, at the very moment of 'election'—the subject and its object represent the relationship between the ego (the subject) and ego ideal (the object)" (1976, pp. 356–57). I suggest that it is because falling in love internalizes the identity of the beloved as an object of empathy that moral standards are singularly mutable when falling in love. The opinions of the beloved contribute to a profound modification of the superego for the duration of the love (Freud, 1925c, p. 257; Sandler, 1960, p. 41; Loewenstein, 1966, p. 311). Kernberg (1993, p. 653) went so far as to suggest that "the interaction of the partners' superego over time results in the forging of a new system, which I am calling the couple's superego." Conversely, moral failure by a loved object may be experienced both as a betrayal and a reason to lower one's own moral standards (in disillusionment, revenge, and so forth). Should a loved object lose moral authority with a child, for example, through a parent's permanent or temporary absence, mental illness, or criminality, the child's inner standards of morality may be lost and delinquency may ensue (A. Freud, 1927, pp. 55–56).

Fenichel (1945) noted that many people's superegos are externally dependent throughout life. "Many persons remain influenced in their behavior and self-esteem not only by what they consider correct themselves but also by the consideration of what others may think" (p. 107). Flugel (1945, pp. 174–75) suggested that the superego's external dependency was not a rare event but the general rule. Rapaport (1958) summarized that the superego depends on interpersonal support.

The superego is a persistent structure, but its conscious parts seem to require stimulus-nutriment. In the lack of nutriment it becomes prone to compromise and corruption, and the greater

their extent, the more mercilessly does the unconscious superego exact its pound of flesh: the unconscious sense of guilt
(Freud, 1923[a]). The maintenance of conscience seems to
require the continuous input of the nourishment readily provided by a stable, traditional environment in which the individual is born, grows up, and ends his life; that is, the stimulus
of the presence, opinions, and memories of the "others" who
have always known him and always will. We seem to choose
the social bonds of marriage, friendship, etc., to secure that
familiar (paternal, maternal) pattern of stimulation which we
need as nutriment for our various superego and ego structures (for example, those which underlie our values and ide-
ologies) (p. 729).

Similar views have been expressed by Rangell (1963, pp. 243–
44; 1980, p. 24), Loewenstein (1966, p. 311), and Blum (in Tyson,
1985, p. 221). To a much greater extent than the id and the ego, *it
is of the very nature of the superego to be engaged in object relations.* Not only are moral standards applied to interpersonal behavior, but interpersonal criteria shape their formulation, maintenance,
and revision.

The superego's responsiveness to other people permits socially
appropriate behavior to be redefined as a person moves from one
group of people to the next. One's moral obligations toward children differ, for example, from one's obligations toward adults. These
and other inconsistencies in people's moral behavior preclude the
possibility that the superego's values possess homogeneity. Rangell
(1980) remarked:

The superego is the least structured and the most fluid of the
three psychic agencies, which is both a blessing and a curse.
Continued accessibility of the superego to outside influences
leaves an individual open to social progress, but it also makes
him prey to the fickle whims of a crowd—from a mild suspension of critical judgment to a sudden and complete regression
to barbarism (p. 24).

The superego may demand consistency as a moral imperative
(p. 29), but it does not observe it. On the other hand, the superego
contains no internal stimulus barriers. It is not subdivided into

preconscious and unconscious as the ego is. For this reason, there can be logical inconsistencies but no psychodynamic conflicts between the superego's values (Rangell, 1963, pp. 223, 229–30). Its lack of internal stimulus barriers permits the superego occasionally to exhibit an extraordinary capacity of synthesis (Glenn, 1989, p. 237) in the formulation of novel values of great power.

Ego Ideals and Interests

When Freud introduced the term "ego ideal" in 1914, it referred to a set of values that the agency that he was then calling "conscience" applies in its deliberations. The ego ideal was both a model for aspiration and a criterion for self-assessment (cf. Morrison, 1983; Milrod, 1990; Tyson & Tyson, 1990, p. 202). Freud changed the term's definition in 1921 to denote the entire psychical agency, to which he continued to attribute the functions of self-observation, conscience (including dream-censorship), and maintaining ideals (Parkin, 1985). Freud later changed terminology yet again. In order to cut short the confusion that he had caused in 1921, Freud referred to the psychical agency as the "superego" from 1923 onward. For the remainder of his life, he wrote of the ideal only in its original sense as a model for aspiration and self assessment.

Freud often discussed the ego ideal in the singular as though its component values were unconsciously organized in the form of an idealized self-image. However, the ego ideal is not a structure but a process; and its manifestations are adequately explained by postulating a great many partial and often inconsistent self-images, rather than a single and cohesive unconscious synthesis. Consider, for example, Erikson's (1977) remarks on the elaboration of ideals that takes place in childhood through the enactment of object relations in play.

> Childhood play, in experimenting with self-images and images of otherness, is most representative of what psychoanalysis calls the *ego-ideal*—that part of ourselves which we can look up to, at least insofar as we can imagine ourselves as ideal actors in an ideal plot, with the appropriate punishment and exclusion of those who do not make the grade. Thus we experiment with and, in a visionary sense, get ready for a *hier-*

archy of ideal and evil roles which, of course, go beyond that which daily life could permit us to engage in. And then, there is always the interplay of the child's imagination with the ritualized fantasy world offered in picture books and in fairy tales, in myths and in parables, which counterpose the best and the worst in human images (p. 101).

The process of play serves, among its other functions, to articulate children's ego ideals. During play, ideals are explored, elaborated, revised, tailored to the self, projected onto others, and adapted to external reality. Play regularly consists of an enactment of empathy with real or imaginary persons who are admired as heroes or condemned as villains. A moral evaluation is always presupposed in the construction in play of "self-images and images of otherness." Where empathy generates conscience through a judgmental, reactive self-evaluation, it generates ego ideals through a judgmental evaluation of the object as admirable and desirable for imitation.

The structural model of the psyche postulates that aggregates of memory have distinctive functions—so that the id has its repressed memories, and the ego has a separate database, while conscience and the ego ideal each have theirs. My model instead assumes that the mind consists of one large database that is differently accessed and utilized by several mental processes. The values attained through conscience are available for use by the ego ideal and vice versa. Freud oversimplified when he wrote of conscience as a measurement of the self against the standard of the ego ideal. All measurements of the self in relation to its ego ideals—all experiences of elation and depression, pride and shame, duty, honor and guilt, acquittal, conviction, obligation, absolution, and so forth—are utilizations of common mnemic data by the process of conscience.

Freud (1914) initially dated the origin of the ego ideal to the first year of life; but when he introduced the term superego, he dated the origin of the entire agency to the resolution of the Oedipus complex in the middle of the sixth year. Nunberg ([1932] 1955) resolved the discrepancy by suggesting that a single psychic agency has two developmental stages. Although Nunberg's suggestion was ignored during Freud's lifetime, it met widespread acceptance in its revival by Annie Reich (1953) and Edith Jacobson (1954b). Jacobson characterized the developmental transition in the sixth year as "the maturation, depersonification and abstraction of the ego ideal . . . and the development of independent, self-critical superego functions and superego demands," that is, conscience (p. 117; cf. 1964, p. 119). Beres (1958, p. 340) added that the superego earlier has a rigidity and obsessiveness that Piaget (1932) termed "moral absolutism." The superego mellows and grows more realistic in its post-Oedipal phase (see also Calef, 1972; Ticho, 1972). Mahon (1991) suggested that these transformations of the superego are by-products of the latency child's cognitive development. The ego ideal originates through empathic role-playing on the basis of sense perceptions of admired individuals. The ego ideal's transition from anthropomorphic roles or concrete ideas of the self into a verbally expressed set of principles, depends on a process of generalization and abstraction that only becomes possible through an advance of cognitive development that occurs around the beginning of latency. Piagetian theory notes a shift at that time from perceptually bound thought to an operational capacity for conceptualization. A child who had formerly assumed that "six baseball bats are bigger in number than six toothpicks" is able to conceptualize the number six in the abstract, and realize its constancy in all cases (Mahon, 1991). This cognitive leap forward in the capacities for generalization and abstraction is crucial to deanthropomorphized ideal formation.

The onset of generalization and abstraction affects several superego processes simultaneously. The role-playing of childhood gives way to games that are played according to rules. The scope of conscience typically grows from a double standard that limits morality to loved objects, to embrace moral integrity in general (A. Freud, 1927, p. 57; [1936] 1966, p. 119; Sandler with Freud, 1985, pp. 225–26). At the same time, the real and imaginary heroes of the ego ideal are developed into abstract principles of virtue.

It is conventional but incorrect to speak of the generalization and abstraction of superego functions as a depersonification (contra: Jacobson, 1954b, 1965; Kernberg, 1975; 1976; 1980; 1984; Rothstein, 1983; Arlow, 1982; 1989). Pruyser (1974) noted that people invariably personify their ideals throughout their lives. In contrast with a value, which can simply be known, an ideal is invariably believed, cherished, endorsed, or hated. To have an ideal is to be engaged in a commitment. It is an object relation and it implies a personification. Because beliefs concerning abstract ideals typically derive from influential interpersonal relations, beliefs function as loved objects even after they have been abstracted from real, external object relations.

The ego is consciously engaged in beliefs, maintaining a love relationship with them much as it engages itself in other persons; it invests itself in beliefs, clings to them, respects and cares for them, and in so doing obtains from them reciprocal satisfactions. A person's love for his beliefs makes him lovable to and beloved by these beliefs, precipitating a constant flow of nutrient energy. Beliefs, like persons, command attention, care, protection, and loyalty (p. 254).

Eagle (1981) independently argued that ego "interests are most meaningfully understood as object relations which involve cognitive and affective links to objects in the world and serve some of the same psychological functions served by more traditionally viewed object relations" (p. 530). In all, I suggest that ego ideals and interests may be deanthropomorphized, but they are never depersonified.

Both anthropomorphic and abstract ideals are the objects of internal object relationships. Their majority are everyday interests rather than dramatically passionate beliefs. The generalization and abstraction of internal objects that begins to occur in the sixth year transforms the manifest contents of the internal objects but does not change their construction as objects. It is reasonable to assume that both anthropomorphic and abstract ideals function as internal objects because they unconsciously remain associated with the real object representations from which they are derived. The values that the superego maintains as ideals are desired as goals because the values are embodied by the people whom the self loves, admires, and seeks to emulate.

Identification and Moral Thinking

Whether moral evaluations are utilized in judgments of conscience or in the entertainment of ego ideals, they are predicated on the unconscious assumption that, in hurting another person, one hurts oneself (Breen, 1986; Merkur, 1999). Abraham (1924) suggested that morality has its foundation in the second half of the first year of life when, following the growth of the first teeth, an infant must learn to inhibit his or her biting to avoid the mother's withdrawal of the breast.

> The first evidence of an instinctual inhibition appears in the shape of morbid anxiety. The process of overcoming the cannibalistic impulses is intimately associated with a sense of guilt which comes into the foreground as a typical inhibitory phenomenon belonging to the third [i.e., oral-biting] stage . . . whose sexual aim is the incorporating of a part of the object (pp. 496–97).

Rado (1928) associated the self-restraint of the infant at the breast with "the close connection between *guilt, atonement* and *forgiveness*" and the establishment of the superego "out of the primary function of self-observation" (pp. 425–26). Melanie Klein (1948) was later to express the subjective sequence as love, guilt, and reparation.

> The urge to undo or repair . . . harm [to the loved object] results from the feeling that the subject has caused it, *i.e.* from guilt. The reparative tendency can, therefore, be considered as a consequence of the sense of guilt (p. 36).

The prosocial consequences of morality have had sufficient evolutionary advantage that our species experiences morality as rational behavior, but when morality is considered logically rather than diagnostically, its coherence proves emotional, not rational. Moral thinking evaluates and treats people as though they were oneself, even in situations when the self neither is dependent on others nor has any reasonable expectation of becoming so. Morality affirms that other people's happiness is to be promoted and their distress minimized even in the absence of reciprocation. Morality is its own reward. It consists of feeling badly about hurting others, and about their pains, and feeling good about benefiting others, and about their happiness.

There is no manifest link between how one makes others feel and how one feels about oneself. There is a manifest relationship, but the logical of the linkage is unconscious. The manifest illogicality of these feelings has historically provided ample scope for explanatory religious speculations that commonly appeal to metaphysical self-interest. One will be rewarded in an afterlife realm, or in a future reincarnation, and so forth. The theme of self-interest in the metaphysical speculations is derived, I suggest, from unconscious fantasies of a different kind of self-interest. Moral behavior is felt to be advantageous and desirable because the beneficiaries of moral behavior are unconsciously imagined to be oneself (Merkur, 1999).

Breen (1986) located the origin of morality in the infant's identification with the mother. To hurt mother is to hurt oneself. This fantasy may originate through a rationalization of the prosocial behavior noted by Abraham, Rado, and Klein; but it is the fantasy, rather than the prosocial behavior alone, that has the power to give origin to morality.

To explain the fantasy of identification, Jacobson (1954a) introduced what is now the accepted position, that "the baby's wish for oneness with the mother, [is] founded on fantasies of oral incorporation of the love object" (p. 242). Freud (1914; 1930) had earlier postulated a neonatal stage of self-object nondifferentiation, but direct infant observation has established that such a developmental phase does not occur (Stern, 1983; 1985). Newborns are never solipsistic. They engage in object relations from birth onward (M. Balint, 1937). An emerging consensus among developmental theorists has consequently reverted to Jacobson's (1954b, p. 98) theory of "wishful fantasies of merging and being one with the mother (breast)" (Keiser, 1962; Gaddini, 1969; Bergmann, 1971; Silverman, 1978; 1979; Silverman, Lachmann, & Milich, 1982; Pine, 1981; 1986; 1990; Harrison, 1986). There never is a time in infancy when the newborn is consciously unable to distinguish self and object. There are, however, unconscious fantasies of merging with mother. It is exclusively in these unconscious fantasies—and never in a healthy infant's realistic knowledge—that subject-object distinctions do not exist or may disappear.

I have elsewhere argued that unconscious merger fantasies development into a schema that subsequently becomes an entire line of cognitive development (Merkur, 1999). For example, identification is not itself moral. Identification is instead consistent with the acute selfishness of narcissistic pathologies. Moral thinking presupposes an adjustment of identification to accommodate or adapt to reality by acknowledging the otherness of other people. Unconscious merger fantasies presumably provide a developmental precursor and foundation for empathy, but no type of morality traces directly and solely to identification fantasies. In moral thinking, there is an emotional link despite the knowledge that self and object differ. The link does not consist of a direct identification. The pleasure taken in being moral is not the same pleasure as the pleasure of receiving moral treatment. The one pleasure has elements of pride, the other of gratitude. These pleasures are already differentiated in the latent content of dreams. Morality is empathic unconsciously as well as consciously.

The capacity for the empathic beginnings of morality arises, I suggest, through the resolution of unconscious merger fantasies, precisely as generalized moral self-regulation arises through the resolution of the unconscious Oedipus complex. Let me underscore this point. Morality originates through an *outgrowing* of identification. Morality effects a compromise between the irrationality of unconscious identification and a realistic perception of other people. Moral reasoning is incommensurate with its ostensible sources in infancy. The transformation of concrete fantasies of being one with the maternal breast—for example, into a sense of fairness toward others—presupposes a developed capacity for metaphorization or, in Piaget's terms, symbolic thought.

Objectifying the Object

Just as the generalization and abstraction of conscience and ego ideals are developmental acquisitions of the sixth year of life, the transformation of unconscious merger fantasies into empathic imagination is consolidated as a developmental milestone no later than the second year (Furer, 1967). The core of the superego, its essential nature as an inborn, hard-wired mental process, must be sought elsewhere.

What needs theoretic explanation is the object-relatedness of superego thinking. The simplest form of conscience consists of an introspective awareness of an emotion that was aroused by the retrospective knowledge that one has caused someone else to feel a particular way. How may we explain object-relatedness? Conscience pertains to interpersonal relations and is partly dependent on other people's values throughout life. Moreover, judgments of conscience have an ego-alien quality. They do not feel introspective; they feel as though they originated outside the self, as judgments on the self by a loved object. Ego ideals too seem external to the self; they are objects of internal object relations.

To address this theoretic puzzle, I begin by noting that object-related thinking is not restricted to the superego's functions of dreams, empathy, conscience, and ego ideals. The psyche's capacity to endow its imaginations with a sense of otherness is the same as its ability to endow its percepts. We have no knowledge directly of external objects. All that sense perception discloses are mental representations of external objects. For example, what we presume to call sight perceptions of other people are synthetic constructions of sensation, overladen with imaginative interpretations, that we happen to see with our eyes open. Shut the eyes and the same representations may still be visible, but then only in memory or imagination.

Mental representations do not possess the significance of objects merely because they are based directly on or at one or more removes from sense perceptions of other people. The psyche plainly possesses the capacity to invest and reinvest mental elements with the significances of self and object. The constellations of sensation, memory, thought, and fantasy that construct the perception of another person may function at one moment as a mental representation of that person. At another moment, the ego may identify with the mental representation, internalizing the materials within its sense of self, so that the self assumes part or all of the other person's identity. During an identification, the mental representation signifies the self and not an object. At yet another moment, the same materials may be assimilated to the superego, causing the introjected materials to assume dynamic form as an active, seemingly autonomous persona or role in superego thinking. Conversely, the self may be projected onto the superego, resulting in an experience of mystical union. The reality of self and object does not determine the significance or construction of their mental representations as self and object. Either order of representation may have either order of significance at any time.

To what may we attribute the psyche's capacity to think in terms of objects? The capacity to represent an object as an object is operative from birth onwards (Stern, 1983; 1985). How do we endow mental representations with the status as objects that empathy and conscience render so very vivid?

Psychoanalytic writers who have addressed the topic have generally suggested that "cathexes" or quantities of "psychic energy" come in two varieties: "narcissistic" or "ego cathexis" and "object cathexis." The application of a type of energy to a mental representation is then said to constitute the representation either as the self or as an object (Jacobson, 1954b; Kohut, 1971, p. 3; Moore, 1975, p. 257). Winnicott (1960b; 1963) expressed the distinction without reference to energy theory by differentiating between the experience of a "subjectively perceived object" and the same object's "objective perception."

The notion of a variable factor has much to recommend it, but reference to psychic energy is unsatisfactory (Holt, 1967). Freud's assumption of a relation between ideas' importance and the quantity of their electrochemical transmissions in the brain was a category mistake. Telephones, telegraphs, radios, and televisions use no more energy to transmit important messages than trivial ones. Energy theory is a fallacy. On occasion, however, it has been used effectively as a metaphor, as in the following discussion of "object cathexis" by Loewald (1978).

> Object cathexis is not the investment of an object with some energy charge, but an organizing mental act [instinctual in origin] that structures available material as an object, i.e., as an entity differentiated and relatively distant from the organizing agent. Such a cathexis creates—and in subsequent, secondary cathecting activities re-creates and reorganizes— the object *qua* object. It is *objectifying* cathexis. Once objects are organized as objects in an initial cathecting act, they are then maintained or restructured in different ways by further objectifying cathexes (p. 195).

Loewald also argued that "narcissistic cathexis" is an investing of a mental representation with the significance of being a mental representation of the self. Through identification, any mental representation may be endowed with the significance of the self. Conversely, any representation may be given the meaning of an object. How are these psychic acts accomplished? Energy theory is a metaphor. What is the nonmetaphoric reality?

To account for the mental constitution of an object as an object, we need to think, I suggest, in terms of mental elements that accomplish self-and-object representations. A consensus has emerged that the internalization of object relations depends on the internalization of complete object relationships and not on object representations alone. Fairbairn (1941) proposed that what is internalized includes, in Kernberg's (1966, p. 25) words, "a self-image component, an object-image component, and both of these components linked with an early affect" (see also Modell, 1958; Sandler & Rosenblatt, 1962; Sutherland, 1963; Loewald, 1973; Dorpat, 1981; Sandler, 1981; Arlow, in Boesky, 1983; Boesky, 1983; Settlage, 1993). Laing (1967) emphasized that the internalizations consist of interpersonal dynamics.

What is 'internalized' are *relations between* persons, things, part-objects, part-persons, not the persons or objects in isolation. . . . What is internalized are not objects as such but *patterns of relationship between human presences.* The more constant patterns of such relationships are what we call family structure. That is to say, the individual does not simply internalize or introject persons, parts of persons, objects or part objects, good or bad breast, penis, mother or father, but the individual incarnates a *group structure.* . . . It is *relations not objects* that are internalized (pp. 111, 114, 118).

What I am proposing is that the perception and memory of self-and-object-in relationship is accomplished, among other ways, by mental elements that record relations and are processed in relational terms.

Let us assume that the psyche has a "default" position, common to both the instincts and the ego, which it assumes unless programmed otherwise. Every mental representation is, by default, a representation of the self and may consequently be treated at any time during life as a "subjectively perceived object" (Winnicott, 1960b, 1963) or "narcissistic selfobject" (Kohut, 1971, p. 3). The evidence of multiple personality disorder proves emphatically, for example, that splits within the ego result, when repressed, in unconscious identifications with the self. No matter how many times the ego may split its representations of the self, what remains is always a self-representation. Splitting does not result in the creation of self-and-object relationships, because the "default" position remains unchanged.

For the mental representation of an object to signify an object, it must be distinguished from the mental representation of the self. Because any mental representation can be invested with the significance of the self, object representation cannot be achieved simply through the representation of another person. *Ex hypothesi* every representation is subject to immediate identification, resulting in a narcissistic self object, unless the default position is altered or qualified. In characterizing an object as "an entity differentiated and relatively distant from the organizing agent," Loewald implied that the representation of an object as an object requires the representation of the object in relationship to the self. I suggest that it is only when the psyche provides a mental representation that is to be identified with the self that a further representation can acquire relationship to the self as its object. The self functions, as it were, as the ground by contrast with which the object appears as a figure. Objectification is accomplished through the mental representation of both self and object in relationship. It is not accomplished through the mental representation of objects alone.

The mental elements that construct objects as objects are rarely self-evident as self-and-object representations because we take the distinction for granted. Just as we lose sight of the ground when attention is focused on a figure, so we may forget the self when we attend to an object. The portion of a self-and-object representation that represents the self is excluded from attention, if not also from consciousness, immediately as it is associated with and anchored in all else that the self and ego are. What attracts attention, because it alone is sufficiently distinctive to remain the conscious figure of attention, are the portions that represent objects.

Innate Knowledge of the Object

The psyche's capacity to construct an object as an object, which I attribute to mental elements that represent self-and-object relationships, is an innate, inborn, autonomous mental function. It is consistent, I suggest, with Melanie Klein's theory that the sucking instinct provides the newborn with an innate knowledge of the breast.

The new-born infant unconsciously feels that an object of unique goodness exists, from which a maximal gratification could be obtained, and . . . this object is the mother's breast. . . .

The fact that at the beginning of post-natal life an unconscious knowledge of the breast exists and that feelings towards the breast are experienced can only be conceived of as a phylogenetic inheritance (Klein, 1952, p. 117).

In explanation of Klein's theory, Bion (1962a, 1962b) suggested that an infant initially has no "conception" of the breast, but has an innate "preconception" that meets its "realization" through the actual encounter with the breast. The innate unconscious knowledge consists of the mental representation of an instinctual urge to seek that on which to suck. The infant does not have an inborn mental image of the breast. The mental representation of the sucking instinct is initially a wish for an object that is not as yet known to be the breast. Because the wish exists, the infant's initial perception of the breast does not come as an incomprehensible discovery, but as the recognition of an object that satisfies the instinct to suck.

Klein's postulation of the infant's inborn knowledge of the breast has generally been resisted by ego psychologists, but the passage of time has made her theory seem modest. In order to account for the complex social interactions in which newborns engage from birth onward, cognitive psychologists have postulate the inborn, genetically determined basis of the infant's knowledge of the mother as an object of communication (Bråten, 1988; Murray, 1991). Theories of this order are logically necessary. The theory of neonatal subject-object nondifferentiation has collapsed. It is untenable that the human mind starts out as a *tabula rasa*. It is neither a discorporeal soul nor an unprogrammed computer. It is an embodied mind, a function of living, organic flesh. The mind is never blank. It first functions or comes into being in a middle stage of gestation within a living organism whose physiological drives shape its desires and so endow it with a modest complement of innate ideas.

Rather than a genetic endowment directly of ideas, it may suffice to postulate an inheritance of physiological instincts that the mind perceives in the form of mental representations. It is not, as Fairbairn (1963, p. 224), claimed that "the ego, and therefore libido, is fundamentally object-seeking." The causal relationship is the inverse. It is because *sexuality seeks an object* that the mental representation of sexuality takes form as a self and an object in relationship.

The mental representation of the sexual object may be understood as a mental representation of another subject, another self. We deal not with an object, but with a second sense of self (compare: Ogden, 1990, pp. 164–65). The sense of self that includes the power of will or conation, we call I—the self or ego. The other sense of self enters into relationship with the ego and seems to the ego to have the dynamism, otherness, and desirability of a higher, more moral, and more ideal sense of one's self.

The reliance of the superego on mental elements that consist of self-and-object relationships determines that the superego's reasoning process pursues two points of view simultaneously. Where the ego is self-occupied, the superego is group minded. It reasons in terms of both empathy and its introspective, reactive evaluation.

Self-Observation

Along with conscience and the ego ideal, self-observation was the third major function that Freud attributed to the superego. Although self-observation is integral to the activity of conscience, the theoretical link between conscience and the ego ideal, on the one side, and self-observation, on the other, is to be found in the superego's function to constitute the object as an object. Relational thinking, the superego's function to think in terms of self-and-object-in-relationship, is the function that generates self-observation.

Self-observation may be understood as the consequence of an innate assignment of a portion of the psyche to represent the object as an object and to reason from its point of view. When the psyche's capacity to endow a mental representation with the significance of an object is applied to mental representations of the self, the self is treated as an object, and self-observation results. Empathy is an effort to imagine an object as though it were a subject. Self-observation is the view of the self that the object is unconsciously imagined to have.

Summary

The superego is responsible, Freud argued, for conscience, ego ideals, and self-observation. Rejecting ego psychology's denial that the superego reasons, I have argued that empathic reasoning underlies both judgments of conscience and the development of ego ideals. The innate core of superego function is, in my view, the representation of the loved object as an object, together with an attendant reasoning process. The reasoning process, which may be termed "relational thinking," generates empathy in its view of the object, but self-observation in its view of the self.

Chapter 3

INSPIRATION

In the previous chapters, I have argued that two unconscious processes—the dream-work and conscience—exhibit an intelligence and wisdom whose existence most psychoanalysts have failed to acknowledge. The present chapter addresses the same oversight in psychoanalytic theory in reference to a third body of data, but the structure of my argument will now be reversed. Creativity is a process whose intelligence is widely acknowledged, but whose unconsciousness psychoanalysts have traditionally denied. Creativity has been attributed to the unconscious in the study of esthetics, but—astoundingly!—not in psychoanalysis.

Psychoanalysts have traditionally puzzled over the creative intelligence exhibited by inspirations in both the arts and the sciences. When Freud ascribed irrational thinking to the system *Ucs.*, he had no criteria for distinguishing the irrationality of psychopathology from any other sort of irrationality. Incoherence and irrationality were characteristic of pathological thought and behavior. They were produced by the *Ucs.* Ergo—so the syllogism went—anything produced by the *Ucs.* would necessarily be both incoherent and pathological. Dreams were harmless nocturnal psychoses. Slips of the tongue were everyday pathologies. Religion was a group obsessional neurosis. And creative artistry was a symptom of neurosis. Classical psychoanalysis did not possess the language with which to say otherwise.

The diagnostic absurdity went uncorrected until Ernst Kris emphasized that fantasying is healthy whenever it proceeds under conscious control. His famous formulation, "regression in the service of the ego" (Kris, 1934) was widely endorsed for its diagnostic significance. An extensive body of clinical findings has since supported Kris's diagnosis by establishing that psychopathology inhibits creativity (Segal, 1952; Kubie, 1953; 1958; Martin, 1956; Berlin, 1960; Greenacre, 1960; Ruitenbeek, 1965; Rubenstein & Levitt, 1980–81; McDougall, 1994).

Kris did not articulate the precise theoretic implications of his phrase until 1950, when he published an essay "On preconscious mental processes." In it, he explained creativity as follows:

The assumption that the ego directs countercathexes against the id is essential to any study of preconscious mental processes; also essential is the assumption that a preconscious process from which the ego withdraws cathexis becomes subject to cathexis with id (mobile) energy and will be drawn into the primary process (the basic assumption of the psychoanalytic theory of dream formation). The reverse (unconscious material becomes preconscious) occurs when id derivatives are cathected with ego energy and become part of preconscious mental processes at a considerable distance from the original impulse. They may do so if changes in the distribution of countercathexis have taken place, e.g., if the level of conflict has been reduced and the id impulse has become more acceptable; also, they may sometimes enter preconscious mental processes at a considerable price in terms of symptoms (p. 306).

We may immediately ignore Kris's recourse to theories of psychic energies and express his basic concepts without reference to them. Kris's model drew on Freud's ideas of dynamic psychic processes while avoiding his static metaphors of topography and structure. Kris imagined the primary and secondary processes as though they were computer programs that share a common database. According to Kris, when conscious thought abandons psychic materials, not only by repressing them, but also by merely neglecting them, the materials become available for unconscious associations with instinctual materials. Structural relocation in the psyche is not involved. Whether the materials are repressed or neglected, they cease to be utilized by the secondary process (i.e., by the ego) and instead become available for processing by the id. As fantasies manifest, the process is reversed. Materials originating through the ego that have secondarily been revised unconsciously by the id will come thirdly to be accessed by preconscious ego functions.

Most psychoanalytic studies of creativity take Kris's model for granted. Greenacre (1957; 1958; 1960) and many subsequent writers underscored the importance of developmental factors by demonstrating the role of infantile experiences in determining both the personalities of creative individuals and the topics that interest them. Both healthy and pathological developmental factors have been noted (Bellak, 1958; F. Deutsch, 1959; Weissman, 1961; 1967; Gedo, 1972; 1979; Noy, 1972; Sonnenfeld-Schiller, 1972; Glenn, 1974; Nass, 1975; Niederland, 1976; Myers, 1979). The range of factors is, however, so very extensive (Shainess, 1989) as to preclude generalization. All manners of positive and negative childhood experiences have been shown to contribute content to creativity. In rare cases when reference was made to inspiration, appeal was made to Kris's theory.

Kris's model is inconsistent, however, with the phenomenology of inspiration. Intelligence and realism are present in creative inspirations when they first manifest.

Inspired Creativity

Inspiration takes its name from the biblical idea of an entrance of the Holy Spirit into the human soul, but the phenomenon is today generally understood in the study of esthetics as a manifestation of unconscious materials. By definition, a creative inspiration "is always accompanied by the 'aha' phenomenon, the feeling of sudden fit, the feeling of closure, a mingled sentiment of surprise and gratification, and elation" (Bellak, 1958, p. 374). A creative inspiration seems subjectively to enter a passive consciousness from without (Lee, 1948). It has the character of a completed pattern or logical structure, yet its manifestation creates a gap in conscious thought by leaping well beyond previous attainments (Patrick, 1937; Cohn, 1968). Despite its speculative character, it is attended by a subjective sense of certainty, of perfect confidence and absolute conviction in its validity (Lee, 1948; Kris, 1950).

Consider, for example, the following testimonies of Albert Einstein, the composer Johannes Brahms, and the British poet laureate John Masefield.

It's a sudden illumination, almost a rapture. Later, to be sure, intelligence analyzes and experiments confirm (or invalidate) the intuition. But initially there is a great forward leap of the imagination (Kirk, 1971, p. 142).

Straightway the ideas flow in upon me, directly from God, and not only do I see distinct themes in my mind's eye but they are clothed in the right forms, harmonies and orchestration. Measure by measure the finished product is revealed to me when I am in those rare, inspired moods (Abell, 1955, p. 21).

This illumination is an intense experience, and so wonderful that it cannot be described. While it lasts, the momentary problem is merged into a dazzlingly clear perception of the entire work in all its detail. In a mood of mental ecstasy, the writer (and sometimes the painter also) perceives what seems to be an unchangeable way of statement, so full, and so insistent, that he cannot set down one half of what there is to utter (Freemantle, 1964, pp. 257–58).

Inspiration consists, in many cases, of the detailed imagination of a complete discovery or finished work of art. Inspiration is not limited to irrational motifs that provide point of departures for industrious labor. In one instance, Masefield reported, "The poem appeared to me in its complete form, with every detail distinct: the opening lines poured out upon the page as fast as I could write them down" (Freemantle, 1964, p. 257). Brahms claimed that "the finished product is revealed to me." The mathematician Henri Poincaré (1903, p. 36) stated, "Ideas rose in crowds. . . . I had only to write out the results."

Creativity does not always involve an experience of inspiration (Bush, 1969; Kligerman, 1972, p. 27; Niederland, 1976, pp. 189–90). Even when it does, the inspiration is only one aspect of a larger process. For purposes of analysis, Wallas (1926) divided inspired creativity into four phases: preparation, incubation, illumination, and verification. Preparations consciously identify a problem and gather materials toward its solution. The ideas are incubated outside consciousness where they undergo development into a solution. Once incubated, the developed ideas erupt into consciousness as inspirations or intuitions in a moment or period of illumination. The final phase, which is often better described as elaboration than verification, begins when the sense of certainty yields to critical analysis and the inspirations are reexamined, tested, revised, crafted, or otherwise employed in conscious reasoning and behavior.

Wallas acknowledged that creative work often involves a considerable number of inspirations that develop concurrently at different paces. Partial solutions may manifest consciously at intervals prior to the culminating inspiration of a definitive solution (Patrick, 1935; 1937; 1938). Single creative projects may involve a series of inspirations that build one on another in sequence (Vinacke, 1952). These several qualifications do not significantly alter the theoretic description of any single inspiration.

Inspiration as Wish-Fulfillment

The process of inspired creativity can be viewed as an instance of wish-fulfillment. The creation of an unsatisfied wish is inherent in the preparation phase of the creative process. Whenever the ego labors unsuccessfully at a problem, it inadvertently formulates an unsatisfied wish for the problem's solution. The phases of incubation and illumination may be understood as the unconscious production and conscious manifestation of a wish-fulfillment that provides a solution to the initial problem. The final phase of elaboration consists at minimum of the integration of the fantasied solution within the ego.

Wish-fulfillment theory solves one of the major theoretic puzzles of creativity: inspiration's originality. A number of writers—almost never psychoanalytic—have attributed the originality to more or less random associations (e.g., Sinnott, 1959, pp. 25–26; Koestler, 1964, p. 119). They imagine the unconscious to be associating all manner of ideas at random at all times. To account for the fact that large quantities of gibberish do not manifest consciously while a person waits for the random emergence of practical solutions to creative problems, these theoreticians are forced to postulate the unconscious operation of a censorship that recognizes and discards gibberish, and so allows only useful ideas to manifest consciously as inspirations. Because psychoanalysts understand free association to be unconsciously directed by instinctual desires, they seldom accept the premise of randomness that this model of creativity entails. A second problem with the general model is how very wasteful it would be for the psyche to generate original ideas at random and be forced to discard their vast majority as being incoherent or, at best, impractical.

One advantage of wish-fulfillment theory is the economy or parsimony of its explanation of creative originality. Freud's theory of the dream-work needs neither revision nor expansion in order to explain originality as a direct process of condensing two ideas and so fashioning a metaphor, analog, or heurism for further incubation. The condensation of an unsatisfied present wish with the memory of a similar wish that was satisfied in the past results in the fantasy of the present wish being fulfilled in the same manner as the past fulfillment. Originality arises through the application of the past circumstance to the present problem. There is recourse to analogy, but not to randomness. Although some analogies may be weak or unusable, none are nonsensical associations of ideas. There is no need to postulate an unconscious censorship that identifies and discards gibberish. There is never any gibberish. There is only imaginative wish-fulfillment.

Inspired creativity cannot simply be assimilated to wish-fulfillment theory without further comment, however. Creativity does not compensate for unsatisfying reality by retreating into fantasy. Unlike the manifest content of dreams, daydreams, and related forms of fantasy, inspired creativity is realistic in content and practical in its problem-solving. Its uses of symbolization do not retreat into incoherence but are somehow reconciled with a sense of reality. Creativity is not limited to the production of analogies that liken one thing to another without allowance for differences. Creativity often takes reality into account and develops symbols and metaphors into workable analogs, heurisms, and models.

Freud (1900) acknowledged that "the most complicated achievements of thought are possible without the assistance of consciousness" (p. 593), but he never adequately accounted for the realistic practicality of inspired creativity. Freud (1908a) compared creative writing with daydreaming, but he offered no account for the enormous differences between the two. Twenty years later, Freud (1928) confessed: "Before the problem of the creative artist analysis must, alas, lay down its arms" (p. 177).

Kris's (1950, p. 306) theory of inspired creativity is similarly incomplete. Kris suggested that when the conscious ego loses interest in psychic materials, the materials are rendered preconscious. They also become available for unconscious development through wish-fulfillment and symbolization. Because preconscious materials are not inherently censorable, once they have been developed into fantasies by means of the dream-work, they may manifest consciously. This general process may commence either spontaneously or as a deliberate, voluntary effort of the conscious ego. Kris's theory fails to account for both the intellectual power and the practicality of creative inspirations.

Other Kinds of Creativity

Because wish-fulfillment theory has not provided a sufficient explanation of creative inspirations, several psychoanalytic writers have approached the puzzle of creativity from other perspectives. Ehrenzweig (1953) and several later writers (e.g., Walkup, 1965; Roland, 1981) noted that creative thinking often proceeds through manipulations not of verbally expressed concepts, but of concrete ideas whose forms are consistent with sense percepts. Academic psychological research on mental imagery later corroborated these findings (Forisha, 1981; Shaw & Belmore, 1982–83). Like verbal ideas, concrete ideas are hypothetical or fictional presentations. They are often representational rather than abstract in form; but Ehrenzweig (1964; 1967) also observed that some scientific thinking utilizes concrete ideas that do not resemble sense percepts but are abstract in form and meaning.

Bush (1969) pressed the case for nonverbal secondary process thinking in creativity, but he conceded to Kris's theory that the invention or acquisition of imagined perceptions presupposes topographic regression of at least momentary duration. Rothenberg (1976b) ingeniously added that secondary process thought is capable of both logic and systematically paradoxical thinking, such as "actively conceiving two or more opposite or antithetical ideas, concepts, or images simultaneously," or "two or more discrete entities occupying the same space" (Rothenberg, 1976a, p. 18).

This entire line of research remains incidental to Wallas's theory. Inspired creativity and concrete secondary process thinking may have equivalent social functions to produce novel ideas. The processes may both be termed imaginative, but they are significantly different psychic phenomena. The existence of conscious reasoning with concrete ideas does not disprove the occurrence of inspiration.

A small number of studies has addressed the theory that beauty arises from the forms or shapes of esthetic objects, as distinct from their contents. In order to account for the artistic creation of formal beauty, Ehrenzweig (1948–49), Arieti (1976), and Deri (1984) attributed an innate knowledge of esthetic forms to the id. The appreciation of shapes as beautiful would then be a genetic endowment. Rose (1980; 1990) argued, however, that the esthetics of forms are acquired developmentally through the ego's experiences of bodily shapes. Once again, we may acknowledge the validity of the line of research, while noting that the theories do not bear on our present concern with instances of creativity that display exceptional intelligence.

Illusions

In commenting on biographical studies of creative personalities, Lee (1948; 1949) emphasized the methodological distinction between psychoanalyses of the latent contents of creative inspirations and theoretic accounts of the inspirations' forms. The contents of different inspirations may have diverse sources in early development yet share a common form or character as inspirations.

One of the few theoreticians who considered inspiration's character as inspirations, Kris (1939) suggested that unconscious manifestations seem subjectively to enter consciousness from without because the secondary process does not contribute to their formation and knows nothing of them until the materials manifest. The ego-alien quality of inspiration, its character of seeming to be a disclosure or revelation to the self from outside it, is a notable feature of inspiration's phenomenology.

Many psychic functions are unconscious, however, including split-off portions of the ego. A conclusive argument of the ego's uninvolvement in inspiration may be based on two other formal characteristics: the certainty and elation that attend its occurrence. The sense of certainty concerns the value of the inspiration; the mood of elation attends the certainty. Both feelings vary in intensity from instance to instance but are otherwise constant features of inspiration's phenomenology. It is not only authors of literary fictions who may feel that they have come upon "an unchangeable way of statement." Einstein (1954) wrote:

> To him who is a discoverer in this field, the products of his imagination appear so necessary and so natural that he regards them, and would like to have them regarded by others, not as creations of thought but as given realities (p. 264).

The certainty and elation are not necessarily valid. Much art fails. Many discoveries and inventions prove mistaken. The certainty and elation are illusory in the psychoanalytic sense of the term, which differs from the term's usage in perception psychology. Freud (1927a) wrote:

> An illusion is not the same thing as an error; nor is it necessarily an error. . . . What is characteristic of illusions is that they are derived from human wishes. . . . Illusions need not necessarily be false—that is to say, unrealizable or in contradiction to reality . . . we call a belief an illusion when a wish-fulfilment is a prominent factor in its motivation, and in doing so we disregard its relation to reality, just as the illusion itself sets no store by verification (pp. 30–31).

Illusions are consciously known to be imaginations yet are endorsed as valid. The endorsement occurs during the immediate experience of the illusions and sometimes also in retrospect. As illusions, Freud (1927a; 1927b; 1930) mentioned the instances of art, religious doctrines, value judgments, and humor. Winnicott (1953; 1966; 1971) broadened the discussion of illusions to include transitional objects, children's play, and culture in general.

In contrast with pathological symptoms, whose fallacies are exempted from reality-testing by the resistance that buttresses their repression, illusions are not fixated. Creative inspirations are always illusory at the moment of their manifestation. However, they become subject to reality-testing shortly thereafter. Reality-testing during the final, elaboration stage of the creative process often shatters the sense of certainty that attends them by disclosing the inspired solutions as valid, if at all, for heuristic purposes only.

In some cases, however, illusions happen to be able to withstand even the most rigorous reality-testing. Writing specifically of religious illusions, Freud (1927a) remarked:

> Religious doctrine . . . allows of a refinement and sublimation of ideas, which make it possible for it to be divested of most of the traces which it bears of primitive and infantile thinking. What then remains is a body of ideas which science no longer contradicts and is unable to disprove (p. 52).

Consider other examples. Empathy and morality are less exotic and more nearly rational instances of illusion. Benefit and harm exist, but do good and evil? Are moral categories extrapolations from prosocial behavior that make unwarranted assumptions about the nature of reality? A parallel argument can be made about the relation of sexual attraction and beauty. The behavioral motivation is real. But is the metaphysical value? Because their reality can be neither proved nor refuted, good, evil, beauty, and ugliness are illusions in the psychoanalytic sense of the term.

Reality-testing can do little more with tenable illusions than to establish the epistemic fact that illusions are illusions: intrapsychic wishful thinking. According to Freud (1927a), illusions are never validated by proof, but only by emotional preferences. Whether the preferences are valid or misplaced, reality-testing is often unable to decide. "Of the reality value of most of them we cannot judge; just as they cannot be proved, so they cannot be refuted" (p. 31).

Because inspirations are illusory, they cannot be attributed to split-off portions of the ego. Illusions are subject to reality-testing, as split-off ego functions are not. Like the hallucinatory quality of dreams, the illusory quality of inspirations is compelling reason to attribute their production to a process outside the ego.

The Objectivity of Creativity

Psychoanalysts have traditionally denied the unconsciousness of creative intelligence, not for lack of evidence, but to avoid the necessity of revising the conventional models of the mind. Clinical studies of dreams, daydreams, and neurotic symptoms led Freud to the conclusion that wish-fulfillment diverts attention from an unsolved problem to a soluble analog without developing a solution to the initial problem. How a flight into fantasy can be transformed into practical success (e.g., in scientific discovery and invention) has remained an unsolved theoretic puzzle.

The originality of creative inspirations may in part be attributed to the novel perspectives that symbolization imparts to all types of fantasy (Alexander, 1948); but the character of a creative inspiration as "a completed pattern or structure" (Cohn, 1968, p. 169) differs from sequential, incremental fantasying about persons, sceneries, and events in dreams, daydreams, hypnagogic states, and so forth. Inspirations erupt into consciousness with complete or nearly completed solutions to practical problems. How does realism enter the process? How is unconscious symbol formation reconciled with the reality principle?

Kris's (1950) theory of "regression in the service of the ego" offers no explanation whatever of the practical rationality of creative inspirations. Kris was stymied by his own attribution of the inspirative character of creative inspirations to their unconscious origin. One of the architects of ego psychology, Kris arrogated all rational intelligence to the ego (Hartmann, Kris, & Loewenstein, 1946). How was he then to account for the intelligence of creativity? If inspirations have an "aha" character because they emerge unexpectedly from the id, inspirations cannot be intelligent. Yet they are!

Building on Kris's (1950) view that the preconscious ego instigates unconscious symbol-formation in both daydreaming and creative inspiration, Kubie (1958) suggested that it must be the preconscious ego that adds coherent reasoning to unconscious symbolism and so transforms fantasy into creative inspiration. Kubie's theory fails, however, because the rational intelligence is already part of the inspiration prior to its manifestation. The ego experiences the incubated materials as inspiration and becomes active in the elaboration phase precisely because it does not contribute rationality during the earlier incubation phase.

Existing superego theories provide no better solution. Conscience has occasionally been implicated in inspired creativity, but only in peripheral or supportive capacities. Melanie Klein (1929) drew attention to the role of conscience in motivating and approving creative inspirations. Although she treated creativity as a symptom of pathology, she maintained that creativity defends against depression, guilt, mourning, and so forth—in all cases, negative derivatives of conscience—through reparation or restoration of the lost or destroyed love object. Lee (1948) suggested that reparation is achieved when the contents of the creative inspiration meet the approval of conscience, which values the inspiration as an ideal. This process of superego approval accounts for both the feeling of elation during the manifestation of an inspiration and the attendant sense of certainty in the validity of the inspiration's contents. Weissman (1969) added that a person's dedication during the elaboration phase of creative activity proceeds more in the service of the ego ideal than in the service of the ego. The interpersonal objects of empathy, conscience, and ego ideals cannot be made to account, however, for the impersonal concerns of creativity in the arts and sciences.

Schachtel (1959) noted that creativity centers "on the object, idea, problem which is the focus of the creative endeavor" (p. 245). There is a world of difference between daydreams, for example, about writing a novel, painting a work of art, or making a scientific discovery, and creative inspirations that contribute actual content to the respective creative endeavors. Freud (1908a) remarked that "His Majesty, the Ego, [is] the Hero . . . of every day-dream" (p. 150). The observation may be extended to dreams, hypnagogic and hypnopompic reveries, hypnotic dreams, hysterical dream states, psychotic hallucinations, and all other fantasies that have narrative structures. Narrative fantasies—for so I collectively term them (Merkur, 1998)—invariably imagine the fulfillment of what Noy (1969) termed "self-centered" ambitions, goals, plans, and desires. Creative inspirations are instead "reality-oriented" (p. 167). Their contents present realistic solutions to practical problems.

The phenomenological distinction is important. The reality-orientation of creativity proceeds from an impersonal or objective perspective. It considers the creative endeavor in its own right as a problem that is to be solved, so far as possible, from an objective point of view. The determination whether any particular wish-fulfillment is to be a self-oriented fantasy or a reality-oriented inspiration depends, I suggest, on the content of the initial wish. In creative inspiration, reality-orientation is introduced in the very formulation of the unsatisfied wish. In contrast with wishes that generate narrative fantasies, wishes that result in creative inspirations are consciously considered from an impersonal, objective perspective before they undergo wish-fulfillment. Daydreams, for example, arise when pondering one's wishes and possible actions, but creative inspirations from thinking about creative projects in their own right. An impersonally considered topic of concern is present in the very wish for a creative solution.

In cases of artistic self-expression, the reality-orientation of creativity may be attributed to the self-observing function of the superego. Weissman (1971) noted the involvement of self-observation in the incubation of creative inspirations:

The superego function of self-observation plays a considerable role in shaping the drive and affective component of creative works. To whatever degree a creative work represents the inner world of its creator, the artist, he must call upon his capacity for self-observation to collect and arrange his unnoticed ideas, feelings and drives in response to both external and internal stimuli (p. 217).

The role of self-observation is unmistakable in cases when creativity is obliged to address the self. In the performing arts and the writing of autobiographies, for example, creative inspirations treat the self impersonally, as though it were the self of another person. Sachs (1942) observed:

The daydreamer is always his own hero, the poet never. Even when he tells his story as though it were about himself and uses a great deal of his own life and character as material, the poet does so in a sense quite different from that of the daydreamer: he is not guided by a wish for self-glorification, but for self-investigation (p. 42).

Self-observation is integral to creativity in the performing arts and autobiographical narrative. It is through the superego that the self "can take itself as an object, can treat itself like other objects, can observe itself, criticize itself, and do Heaven knows what with itself" (Freud, 1933, p. 58). Not only does self-observation treat the self as an object, but it regularly induces a measure of realism or objectivity with regard to the self (Sterba, 1934; Loewenstein, 1963; Grossman, 1982). By relativizing the self as one person among many, the psyche is able to engage in interpersonal relations on a more realistic basis than the ego is able to produce on its own.

The objectivity of creative work in science and technology may be interpreted in parallel. The impersonal, disinterested objectivity of creative inspirations that pertain to the arts is consistent with the impersonal, disinterested objectivity of creative inspirations that pertain to the sciences, technology, or any other field of endeavor (Slochower, 1965). Although the concept of "self-observation" cannot reasonably be stretched to fit scientific topics, there is no reason to suppose that the superego's observing function is limited to observations of the self. The superego, I have argued, has the innate functions of representing the object as an object and reasoning from its point of view. The superego's observing function should not be thought to be limited to self-observation. Self-observation is an application to the special case of the self, of a general capacity to imagine the perspective of the loved object. Observations from the imagined perspective of the object are not made only of the self. Similarly imaginative observations are also routinely made of the balance of reality. The superego applies its distinctive perspective to the observation of the perceptible world. When the superego's observing function addresses mental representations of external reality, it is external reality that is observed from its impartial, disinterested, or "reality-oriented" perspective.

The superego's observing function, which accomplishes both self-observation and objectivity, is an inherently imaginative activity. Objectivity is not a perception of reality but an imagination concerning a hypothetical perception of reality that is inherently and necessarily impossible for any human being ever to achieve. All that any of us ever know, we know in our minds as subjective beings. What we know exhibits regularities that lead us to believe that the universe exists objectively and conforms with objectively existing natural laws; but none of us can directly experience an objective perspective, except as an imagination or as an idea abstracted from imagination.

To its imaginary objective perspective, the superego adds a complementary mode of imaginative reasoning. Whenever the superego reasons about objects, for example, in producing empathy, it both constructs objects as objects and maintains the constructions throughout its reasoning process. In maintaining the distinction between self and object over a period of time, the relational thinking of the superego develops two lines of reasoning simultaneously. One line of thought imagines the perspective of the object; the other evaluates the self's reactions to the object. Creative inspirations in the arts and sciences presumably employ a similarly double line of reasoning that happens to address impersonal rather than interpersonal objects (cf. Koestler, 1964). Instead of empathy, there is an incubation process that develops an initial condensation into a workable creative solution.

Value Judgment

The superego evidently augments its relational thinking with a capacity for reality-testing. For example, in its function as the sleep vigil, the superego enables a sleeping mother to recognize and respond to her baby's cry, while ignoring all other sounds that she hears in the night.

On the other hand, the superego does not deploy its reality-testing capacity in the same manner as the ego does. The rational intelligence of creative inspirations is plainly not a form of secondary process thought. Whatever reasoning process causes inspirations to be practical or realistic differs from the ego's reality-testing. Unlike the ego, which ponders whether mental presentations represent reality or not, the superego produces illusions. The superego is not limited to the factual. It is free to produce both illusions that reality-testing will falsify and illusions that can neither be proved nor refuted.

The superego's mode of reasoning and decision-making may be said to conform with a value principle. It is as though the superego combined the pleasure principle of the id with the reality principle of the ego, from the perspective of its imagined objectivity. The result is the illusion that pleasure has objective reality as a value.

Volney Gay (1992) developed a general theory of value-formation by building on J. J. Gibson's (1979) theory that every perception includes the estimation of an "affordance." For example, the perception of a gap in a fence includes an estimation of its affordance of passage; the estimation is relative to the body size of the individual person or animal that makes the perception. Gay (1992) suggested that "Gibson proposes two seemingly contradictory theses: (1) perceiving an affordance is a value-laden process, and (2) the value perceived is *not* a product of the animal's internal state (which varies) but of the animal's relationship to the perceptible world (which does not vary)" (p. 195).

Gibson advanced his concept of affordances in the context of perception and motor action. Gay introduced the parallel concept of "emotional affordances."

Emotional affordances [EA] are "constant" aspects of the infant-parent interactions. If EA are analogous to visual affordances, then they should be discoverable at some level of observational science. Just as we nonconsciously gauge visual affordances, we must also *nonconsciously gauge emotional affordances*. . . .

To discover what count as EA in a particular person's life one must observe how that person acts and interacts with the person's environment. These observational records and assessments may not match the actor's self-understanding nor the "correct" view of themselves maintained by others (pp. 212–13).

For Gay, emotional affordances are realistic, objectively warranted, and unvarying value-judgments that "pertain to the quality of relationship between the other person and ourselves" (p. 244).

Having developed his theory by reference to the emotional affordances of human relationships, Gay proceeded to the topic of sublimation, which he explained as the representation of emotional affordances in art and other cultural artifacts. "Sublimation names creative processes by which persons preserve insights into the human world, a world whose qualities are represented in the work of art" (p. 241). Gay's theory of sublimation is a theory of empathy in the original esthetic context of the term. Where interpersonal empathy consists of creative inspiration regarding the feelings of another person, esthetic empathy involves a parallel imagining of the feelings implied by a work of art—that is, the feelings that moved the artist to create the artwork as it is. Not only may people at different stages of life imagine that different feelings are implied by single works of art, but different works of art may evoke feelings in single people, at single times of their lives, that were acquired at different stages of their past development.

The evaluation of the emotional affordances in nature may similarly be comprehended as a subcategory of empathy. Whether emotional affordances pertain to people, animals, or natural phenomena, a consistent practice of empathy may be postulated. Conscience applies empathy to people. Esthetic empathy depends on imagining the feelings imparted to a work of art by its creator. The emotional affordances in nature may be explained in parallel as imaginations of the feelings imparted to works of nature, as though by a creator.

In order to maximize the value of an inspiration, the superego utilizes its reality-testing to maximize the inspiration's practicality. The incubation of creative inspirations in the arts deploys reality-testing in the service of esthetic empathy; the incubation of creativity in science, in the service of empathy with an unconsciously anthropic cosmos (see Merkur, 1999, pp. 34–41). In all cases, empathic imagination is integral to the production of illusions. An illusion is most complete and its value greatest when it cannot be falsified by reality-testing and must instead be considered tenable. In art, where originality may be valued as an end in itself, the rationality of inspiration may be expressed more as coherence than as logicality. In science, where a premium is placed on truth, logicality is privileged, but so too is elegance.

Summary

Accepting from Kris (1934) that the originality of creative inspirations is due to the condensation of unrelated ideas through unconscious symbol formation, I have drawn attention to the unconscious intelligence and practical realism postulated by Wallas's (1926) model of creativity. Inspirations derive both their immense database and their ego-alien quality as inspirations from the unconscious, but their intelligence and practicality also require account.

Building on the views of Weissman (1971) and Sachs (1942), who implicated self-observation in creative self-expression, I have argued that the "reality orientation" of creativity (Noy, 1969) is a product of the superego's representation of the perspective of the object. Even though inspirations have an illusory nature or quality, inspirations remain practical and realistic in order to maximize their value as determined through empathic thinking. Whether empathy is interpersonal, as in dreams and conscience, or either fictional or naturalistic, as in creative inspirations, empathy is the basis of value formation.

Chapter 4

METAPHOR AS A TERTIARY PROCESS

A gap in theory remains to be closed. In Chapter One, I was content to demonstrate that the dream censorship performs the whole of the dream-work: both the symbol formation noted by Freud (1900) and the problem-solving empathic thinking that French and Fromm (1964) demonstrated. The prognostic function in dreams provided the point of entry for my review of the classical superego functions in Chapter Two. I made no attempt there to explain how the prognostic function, empathy, conscience, ego ideals, self-observation, and objectifying the object are accomplished by the same psychic agency that performs symbolization. The same question has also arisen with respect to creativity. The superego has traditionally been connected with ethics and values. How does it also accomplish symbol-formation and creativity? We know that it does so, but how does it do so? What is the point of contact between its interpersonal and impersonal functions? What is the underlying common function at the superego's core?

To answer this question, let me approach the problem from a radically different perspective.

The Primary and Secondary Processes

In *The Interpretation of Dreams*, Freud (1900) suggested that the psyche performs two fundamentally different types of thinking. He termed them the "primary" and "secondary processes" (p. 598). Conceiving of the psyche, for heuristic purposes, on the model of an electrical machine, he suggested that the primary process "is built upon the plan of a reflex apparatus." It responds to "excitation . . . felt as unpleasure . . . that . . . sets the apparatus in action with a view to repeating the [past] experience of satisfaction, which involved a diminution of excitation and was felt as pleasure." The primary process reacts to stimuli, but it has no functions that require consciousness and it proceeds wholly unconsciously. Because the exclusive motivation of the primary process is to seek pleasure, Freud said that it was governed by the pleasure principle.

Consciousness was intrinsic, however, to a second process that "diverted the excitation arising from the need [to seek pleasure] along a roundabout path which ultimately, by means of a voluntary movement, altered the external world in such a way that it became possible to arrive at a real perception of the object of satisfaction" (pp. 598–99). Due to the secondary process's cognizance of and conformance with the dictates of external reality, Freud (1911) said that it was governed by the reality principle.

Freud's (1900, pp. 598–99) distinction between a "perception" by the primary process and a "real perception" by the secondary process was obscure, and he made another stab at phrasing his concept a few pages later.

> The primary process endeavours to bring about a discharge of excitation in order that, with the help of the amount of excitation thus accumulated, it may establish a 'perceptual identity'. The secondary process, however, has abandoned this intention and taken on another in its place—the establishment of a 'thought identity'. All thinking is no more than a circuitous path from the memory of a satisfaction (a memory which has been adopted as a purposive idea) to an identical cathexis of the same memory (p. 602).

To make sense of this difficult passage, I suggest that Freud's concept of the primary process was largely but not entirely a mechanistic rephrasing of the animal soul of Aristotlean psychology. Freud's familiarity with the details of Aristotle's model may safely be assumed. He took six courses at the University of Vienna in the

1870s with the philosopher Franz Brentano, who had earlier published a monograph on *The Psychology of Aristotle* (1867).
In his treatise *On the Soul*, Aristotle had divided the psyche
into six faculties. The nutritive faculty was co-extensive with life.
It was found in both plants and animals, and it governed decay,
growth, and reproduction. The capacity for sensation, by which
Aristotle defined animal life, invariably coincided with the further
faculties of local movement, imagination, and appetite. "Where there
is sensation, there is also pleasure and pain and, where these,
necessarily also desire" (*On the Soul*, 2.2) "Inasmuch as an animal
is capable of appetite it is capable of self-movement; it is not capable of appetite without possessing imagination" (3.10). Appetite
has no raison d'être unless it can motivate local movement; appetite also implies a capacity for imagining the object of desire.

The soul's final and highest faculty, which Aristotle recognized
in only a limited group of animal species, was reflective thought
(2.3). Freud termed it the secondary process.

In reconceptualizing Aristotle's faculty psychology as a dynamic
process of psychological conflict, Freud recognized that the four
interrelated faculties of animal souls—sensation, appetite, sensory
imagination, and local movement—collectively form a single process that is known to neurology as a reflex. Consider, for example,
a single-celled bacterium with a whip-like flagellum. The function
of the tail to propel the bacterium toward a food supply is instigated, first by a function that senses the presence of food and
second by an intermediating function that reacts to the sensation
by triggering the motor mechanism. For Aristotle, the intermediating function constituted an appetite for food. Freud instead termed
it an instinct.

Where Aristotle had been willing to recognize psychical activity
in the metabolic processes of plants, Freud was not. Freud was also
unwilling to consider the appetitive faculty a dimension of psyche,
rather than soma. For Freud, even the simplest form of thought
incorporates memory and learning. Freud's primary process can be
understood as a dynamic reconceptualization of Aristotle's account
of sensation, appetite, imagination, and local movement, to which
the functions of memory and learning have been added. Consider
the example of spontaneous sexual arousal at the sight of an attractive person. Arousal always happens unconsciously. Consciousness

may be involved in giving oneself permission to indulge the moment and become aroused, or in engaging in self-stimulation in order to encourage arousal. However, the actual process or processes by which sight results in arousal—all the subterranean links between seeing someone and discovering oneself to be in a state of arousal—proceed without the activity of consciousness. They are intrinsically unconscious. They cannot be conscious. Consciousness may know both the attractive sight and the consequence of being aroused, but the process by which the sight leads to physiological arousal remains outside consciousness, as an unobserved and mysterious process that we ascribe to bodily instinct. The instinct is not unthinking, however. Sexual arousal has an inborn component, but it also integrates learning. Some sights are found arousing when others are not because the sexual instincts have learned to recognize some sights as attractive, but others not. To the extent that sexual arousal incorporates a knowledge of genders, primary and secondary sexual characteristics, standards of attractiveness in deportment, grooming, and clothing, and so forth, sexual arousal includes a learned component. Reflexes and other responses whose complexity compares with sexual arousal interrupt the sequence of sensation, appetite, and motor response with further functions that accommodate learning by involving capacities for memory and the matching of sensations with memories. The sequence of sensation, memory, appetite, and motor response, which occurs, for example, not only in sexual arousal but also in all cases of imprint conditioning, was the simplest information process that Freud discussed as psychological.

Freud used the term "perceptual identity" to describe the association of a sensation with the memory of a similar sensation. A perceptual identity occurs when the equivalence of two sensations is established through their comparison; the process of identification constitutes an act of *recognition*. This primary process of recognizing perceptions is able to proceed unconsciously. It can occur consciously, but it has no need of consciousness in order to be performed.

More sophisticated reflexes instead require consciousness. Consider, for example, Pavlov's famous experiment of ringing a bell whenever a dog ate, until the dog would salivate at the sound of the bell even in the absence of food. Here again learning and memory were at work. What was learned was a historical, rote association of two perceptual recognitions. There was no necessary physiochemical chain of causality linking the sensations of taste and sound. The biochemistries of the two sensations were independent. One involved ears, the other eyes. The two sets of perceptual recognitions pertained to different objects: food and a bell. The mental association of the two recognitions was historical. The association had its basis in coincidence, not in perceptual identity. The coincidence was evident to neither taste recognition nor sound recognition alone. In some manner, the two sequences of physiochemical causality, the sensation and recognition of the food and the sensation and recognition of the bell, were so brought together that their *juxtaposition* became evident to a unified psychic process. This unified or, more precisely, unifying psychic process was first identified by Avicenna, the medieval Muslim Aristotlean philosopher, who termed it the "common sense" (Wolfson, 1935; Harvey 1975). We today call it consciousness.

Consciousness is an "observing function" (Miller, Isaacs, & Haggard, 1965) that is able to perceive different perceptual recognitions simultaneously, as is the condition of its unifying, juxtaposing, or synthetic function (Nunberg, 1931). By perceiving discrete sensations simultaneously, consciousness is able to effect a synthesis by relating the sensations to each other (cf. Baars & McGovern, 1996, pp. 71–72). The synthesis constitutes an intrinsically more complex order of thought. The psychic juxtaposition or synthesis of a plurality of perceptual identities makes possible or constitutes an inherently more realistic appreciation of a physical event, which Freud termed its "real perception."

The juxtaposition proceeds on a basis that Freud termed a "thought identity." The juxtaposition of the different perceptual recognitions has a cumulative effect on their meaning. Each recognition acquires meaning that properly belongs to the other. In the case of Pavlov's dog, the sense recognitions of the bell and the food remained distinct, but their juxtaposition invested them with meanings that they borrowed from each other. The dog salivated because the sound recognition came to share the meaning of the taste recognition. The sound of the bell became a signal of the taste of the food. Conversely, the taste acquired the bell as its accoutrement.

Through their exchange of meanings, the mental elements of a "thought identity" cease to be a plurality of perceptual identities alone. They acquire a cognitive element that is not sensory but is, as Freud recognized, distinctive of a higher order of thought. Bells may exist physically in the absence of thought, but their function as signals does not. The sensations of the primary process can recognize things as being what they are; but a higher order of thought is needed before things can be treated as signifying something other than themselves. For secondary process thought to occur, two conditions must be met. Separate perceptual identities must be (1) brought together in a single, unifying perception (which is consciousness), and (2) augmented with meanings borrowed from each other. The first function, juxtaposition, may be considered an aspect of the synthetic function that Nunberg (1931) ascribed to the ego.

The logical achievements of the secondary process are consequences of its ubiquitous process of testing the accuracy of mental representations. Reality-testing, as the process is termed, consists at bottom of the repeated performance of the simple but ubiquitous process of negation or, as we should today say, falsification. "The function of judgement is concerned in the main with two sorts of decisions. It affirms or disaffirms the possession by a thing of a particular attribute; and it asserts or disputes that a presentation has an existence in reality" (Freud, 1925a, p. 236). Is a thing present or not? Is a thing real or not? By testing the apparent correspondence of mental representations to external reality, the secondary process comes to infer a large body of conclusions regarding reality.

Reality-testing is the only psychological operation that is necessary to account for the accomplishment of logic by secondary process thought. Logic is not an inborn mental function. As studies of cognitive development amply prove, logic is possessed by different people to differing degrees and extents at different times in their lives, because logic is acquired through learning. The logical principle of noncontradiction, on which all rationality depends, corresponds to and arises in reflection of the perceived reality of the world. Because everything that is perceptible is itself and is not anything other than itself, no perception can contradict another. Neither can their realistic mental representations. It is not necessary to argue that logic is an innate or hard-wired mental function. Its principles can be learned through trial and error by every infant who is able to reality-test.

Synecdoche, Metonymy, and Metaphor

When Freud (1923a) renamed the primary and secondary processes, respectively, as the id and the ego, he did not treat the superego as a tertiary process. He termed it "a grade in the ego, a differentiation within the ego" (p. 28). I have suggested, however, that the superego has an inborn function to represent the loved object, among other means, through an inborn capacity to invest mental representations with the significance of objects. How is the superego to be conceptualized as a tertiary process?

Let us return to Freud's notions of perceptual and thought identities. A perceptual identity may be regarded as a very simple type of semiotic function. Consider, for example, a limited sensation, such as the sight of a person, that is associated with memories of more extensive sensations, for example, the sight of a person who was sexually attractive, such that the resultant association triggers a motor or other physiological reflex, such as arousal. In the semiotic idiom of de Saussure, the limited sensation may be said to function as a *signifier*, while the memories of extensive sensations are the *signified*. A perceptual identity is a psychological analog of the literary trope that is termed *synecdoche*, "by which a more comprehensive term is used for a less comprehensive term, or *vice versa*, as part for whole, or whole for part" (*Oxford English Dictionary*). Perceptual identities are analogs of the subset of synecdoche that conforms to the principle *pars pro toto*, the part for the whole. The sight of a person is a part, whose whole consists of a comparable sight that is linked in memory with the idea of sexual attraction. Whether one wishes to call a perceptual identity a sign, symbol, or representation, there is nothing metaphoric about it. In matching parts with wholes, the primary process establishes perceptual identities.

Secondary process thought can also be conceptualized in semiotic terms. In Pavlov's experiment, the sound perception was the signifier, of which the taste perception was the signified. Because the secondary process involves a coincidental relation among its perceptions, its semiotic elements are not limited to synecdoche. Thought identities are the psychological equivalents of the literary trope that is termed *metonymy*, "in which . . . an . . . adjunct is substituted for . . . the thing meant" (*OED*). For Pavlov's dog, the sound of the bell was a discrete or autonomous reality. However, its re-peated juxtaposition with food, as an adjunct to the perception of food, permitted it to signify food. This capacity for signification by metonymy also makes more versatile actions possible. When the bell sounded, Pavlov's dog not only salivated, it also looked and sniffed about in search of the expected food. It treated the bell as a signal of food and undertook voluntary actions on its basis. This independence of thought and action from mere reflex is presumably made possible precisely by the semiotic reliance on metonymy. When perceptions can be assigned meanings other than their own, they can also be detached from the sensory events that gave rise to them. The percepts then become available for use as mental ele-ments with diverse mental functions.

The differences between synecdoche and metonymy will also explain the difference between the pleasure and reality principles. Because the primary process works with synecdoche, its intellec-tual operations are limited to the performance of recognition or matching. Matching examines whether a sensation belongs to a category that triggers an instinctually determined response. There is no opportunity to do anything that is not instinctually pleasur-able, because synecdoche cannot entertain any such concept. The synecdoche of the primary process is limited in its intellectual reach to phenomena that straddle the transition from soma to psyche, and psyche to soma: sensation, instincts, unconscious reflexes, and psychosomatic processes. Because the primary process shares a common database with higher mental processes, it has access to mental elements that it cannot form. It understands them only imperfectly in a fashion that is consistent with its own pleasure-driven level of synecdochic function.

In a similar fashion, the intellectual capacity of the secondary process accomplishes reality-testing because it thinks with mental elements that are metonyms. The capacity for metonymic thought brings reality under consideration. Because the secondary process juxtaposes different sensations to form metonyms, single percep-tions may be the signifiers of different metonyms and so have multiple meanings. The conceptual versatility makes reality-test-ing both possible and necessary. When a perception and its mean-ing are matched or recognized, the function of the signifier as a signifier, its validity or correspondence to the reality that is its meaning, is either confirmed or falsified. Metonym's access to reality serves also as a limitation. Metonyms exploit the versatility of conscious juxtapositions, but their dependence on concrete historical juxtapositions places a limitation on their intellectual reach. The secondary process is committed to the real because the only alternative that it can conceptualize is the false.

A significantly different order of semiotic activity may be attributed to the superego. Its function was originally noted in the context of dreams. Freud (1901a, p. 69) remarked that "the dream-thoughts ... are not clothed in the prosaic language usually employed by our thought, but are on the contrary represented symbolically by means of similes and metaphors, in images resembling those of poetic speech." Freud's observation was explored at length by Sharpe (1937, pp. 19–30), who demonstrated that the symbols of dreams exhibit the range of images and devices that students of literature term "poetic diction." The devices include similes, personal metaphors, implied metaphors, and other sorts of analogy. Similar observations have since been made by experimental dream researchers (Ullman, 1969) and both linguists and literary critics (for references, see Spiro, 1993, p. 17).

In clinical practice, psychoanalysts traditionally interpreted metaphors as though they were dreams and explained the id derivatives as manifestations of unconscious fantasies (Arlow, 1969, p. 7; Reider, 1972, p. 468). Theoretic interest in metaphoric thinking was introduced by specialists in other disciplines. Historians of science established that scientific discoveries are often attained in the form of metaphors that may or may not be revised to become analogs, heurisms, and models (Hesse, 1970; Barbour, 1974; Leatherdale, 1974; MacCormac, 1976; Leary, 1990). The metaphors, analogs, or models are not limited to single images or symbols, but involve a capacity for "logical analogy" (Langer, 1957) or "imaginative rationality" (Lakoff & Johnson, 1980, p. 193).

Championing what had previously been a minority position in philosophy and linguistics, Lakoff and Johnson (1980) persuasively argued that metaphors should not be considered mere figures of speech, but instead form a very large component of everyone's ordinary thought. Many ideas exist only in metaphor. Perceptible phenomena can be thought about and discussed nonmetaphorically, but metaphor is a sine qua non for abstract thought (Thomas,

1969, pp. 25, 31–32; Lakoff, 1993, p. 205). Time, life, causation, and many other realities, or aspects of them, cannot be conceptualized without use of metaphor. Lacan (1957, p. 175) suggested, for example, an intrinsic link of "metaphor to the question of being and metonymy to its lack."

For purposes of brevity, I shall follow Lakoff and Johnson (1980) in referring summarily to the psychological analogs of poetic diction as metaphoric thinking. In literature, a metaphor is "the figure of speech in which a name or descriptive term is transferred to some object to which it is not properly applicable" (*OED*). Although the displacement of meaning from one mental representation to another may be phrased in a variety of subtly differentiated manners that students of literature and linguistics categorize separately, metaphoric thinking is a single underlying process (Burnshaw, 1970; Wheelwright, 1962, p. 71; Lakoff & Johnson, 1980). For example, in the simile "rage is like fire," the term "fire" refers to natural fire and the element that rage and fire have in common is unmentioned. In the metaphor "rage is a fire," the term "fire" refers to the common element and it is natural fire that goes unnamed. Both literary tropes depend, however, on the same psychic process, which develops a novel concept (which may or may not be named) by bringing two dissimilar concepts into relation (whether both are named or not). As long as we address the psychic process while treating its verbalization as an independent variable, use of a single term will suffice for its discussion.

Psychoanalysts arrived at a complementary understanding by reflecting not on literature and language, but on clinical phenomena. Arlow (1979) generalized that "metaphor can be understood . . . as a fundamental aspect of how human thought integrates experience and organizes reality" (p. 368; see also Melnick, 1977). Commenting on Freud's analysis of anal character traits, Arlow (1979, p. 375) suggested that "people with anal personalities categorize their experiences in terms of a metaphor relating to feces. Things are either clean or dirty, valuable or useless, to be retained or expelled, in the proper place or not, at the proper time or not, etc." Leavy (1973, p. 327) cited the parallel phenomena of orality as evidence that metaphoric thought can be preverbal. "Transference interpretations establish the contextual relations of the metaphors: the fantasied presence in the mouth of nipple, or food, or penis, or magical power, or knowledge. Sensation in the mouth, and also images, including fantasies in the visual modality, existed before any words could have designated them."

Psychoanalysis has itself been considered a metaphoric enterprise. Wright (1976, p. 98) described a symptom as "an abortive metaphor that stops below the level of speech." Therapy consists of its verbal articulation. "The undoing of a symptom is in part the creation of *metaphor* from symptom." I would prefer to state that symptoms are metaphors that are not consciously known as such; interpretation brings their latent metaphoricity to consciousness.

Arlow (1979) articulated several general implications of recognizing symbols as metaphors.

> Psychoanalysis is essentially a metaphorical enterprise. The patient addresses the analyst metaphorically, the analyst listens and understands in a corresponding manner. . . . The transference in the psychoanalytic situation represents a metaphorical misapprehension of the relationship to the analyst. The patient says, feels, and thinks one thing about a specific person, the analyst, while really meaning another person, an object from childhood. Thus meaning is carried over from one set of situations, from experiences or fantasies of the early years, to another situation, a current therapeutic interaction in which the old significations are meaningless and irrelevant. Transference in the analytic situation is a particularly intense, lived-out metaphor of the patient's neurosis (pp. 373–74, 382).

Borbely (1998, p. 924) concluded that "trauma leads to a degradation of metaphorical processes" whereas "interpretation uses the metaphorical process in the analysand as well as in the analyst in order to restore the diminished metaphor capacity."

Neither the id nor the ego can logically be held responsible for metaphoric thinking (contra: Roland, 1972; Wright, 1976; Rogers, 1978; Borbely, 1998). Metaphors are symbols that are known to be such. The knowledge may be unconscious, but it is always present. Dreams, for example, are metaphoric, but their metaphoricity is not ordinarily evident during dreaming. A task of waking interpretation is usually necessary before the ego can grasp the metaphoricity that the dream censorship has unconsciously known all along. The self-evidence of metaphors as metaphors presupposes a simultaneous knowledge of metaphors' manifest and latent content. Metaphors can be known as metaphors only to a process that is able to think of both the signifier and the signified simultaneously. The waking ego achieves a simultaneous perception whenever it successfully interprets a symbol and recognizes it as a metaphor. The unconscious occurrence of metaphor as the essential nature of dream symbolism indicates that a similarly simultaneous knowledge can also occur unconsciously. Symbol-formation is a psychical process that is able to join repressed materials with preconscious ego materials, as the signified and signifiers of single signs. Neither the id nor the ego has such a capacity; but the dream censorship forms symbols routinely.

To account for metaphoric thinking, it is necessary to postulate the existence of a process of unconscious thought whose intellectual reach exceeds the limitations of both the primary and secondary processes. Because it can know both repressed and conscious materials simultaneously, its database is greater; but its thinking power is greater too. The relation of the signified to the signifier in metaphoric thinking is limited neither by instinct nor by conscious perception. Where primary process synecdoche signifies a perceptible thing by reference to its part, and secondary process metonymy signifies a perceptible thing in terms of another perceptible thing that was consciously perceived simultaneously, metaphor can associate one kind of thing with another on the basis of their association merely in thought. Synecdoche and metonymy are limited to real objects of sense perception, unconscious and conscious. Metaphors can bring anything that is thinkable into a semiotic relation as signifier and signified. Metaphors can address the perceptible phenomena that are subject to synecdoche and metonymy, but metaphors can also pertain to objects exclusively of thought.

Because the association of signified and signifier in metaphors extends to anything thinkable, the scope of metaphor is potentially unlimited. Metaphor is not restricted to parts that signify the whole, nor to perceptions that happen to be juxtaposed historically. There are no limitations on metaphor. In metaphors, any signifier can signify any signified. Metaphors can be concrete and representational; but metaphoric thinking can also be fanciful, imaginary, arbitrary, nonrepresentational, or abstract. The versatility of metaphor makes possible both a potentially high order of intelligence and the conceptualization of abstract and/or metaphysical concepts. Concrete signifiers, used as metaphors, permit the construction of the purely intellectual (Thomas, 1969; Lakoff, 1993; Leddy, 1995). The same conditions also permit the entertainment of both the fictional and the imaginary.

Language may be a further intellectual achievement of the capacity for metaphor. When the versatility of metaphor generates signifiers that are nonrepresentational or abstract (in the sense that abstract art is abstract), metaphoric thinking makes language possible. The sounds of which spoken words are composed have no intrinsic meaning but instead bear an arbitrary relation to the words' meanings. Some few phonemes are onomatopoeic; the vast majority are nonrepresentational or abstract. Because the association of phonemes with their meanings occurs in thought, rather than either conscious perception or unconscious instinct, the association may be described as metaphoric—arguably in an extended sense of the term. Although literary metaphors are a subcategory of linguistic activity, language itself is a subdivision of metaphoric thought that makes use of abstract signifiers.

That the psyche processes language in two separate manners was suggested by the linguist Roman Jakobson (1956), who demonstrated that there are two types of aphasia. In the one, it is primarily the capacity for metonymy that is lost; in the other, it is the capacity for metaphor. Presumably the secondary process cannot accomplish metaphoric thinking but can make use of the metaphors that it happens to learn. The relation between the signifier and the signified is figurative in a metaphor; but once such a relationship has been established, no matter how arbitrarily, the relation can be learned by rote. The secondary process does not need to understand the metaphor as metaphor. It treats it as though it were a metonym; but it is able to reason with it when it does so. The reduction of a tertiary process metaphor to a secondary process metonym proceeds, however, at a cost of concretizing or reifying the metaphor. It ceases to be felt to be heuristic and comes instead to be treated as an accurate reflection or representation of the signified.

Metaphor and the Return of the Repressed

The versatility of metaphor also makes displacement possible. Metonyms are subject to repression because the association of the signifier to the signified in a metonym originates through the conscious perception of a single event. If the event was traumatic, both the signifier and the signified are subject to repression. With metaphors, circumstances are otherwise. When anything can signify anything, a signifier can always be generated that can successfully evade repression and bring traumatic materials to consciousness in symbolic form.

Freud was wrong to treat displacements as irrational decay products of psychic conflict that divert overly energetic unconscious materials from consciousness. Psychic energy is a metaphor whose reification cannot logically be made to account for the "return of the repressed." There is no "unbound energy" in the psyche. Displacements are not broken, decay products of its collision with stimulus barriers. Displacements are coherent mental elements. They mediate repressed materials to consciousness.

The ego has several stimulus barriers that protect the ego's conscious decision-making processes from a variety of unpleasures: boredom, preoccupation with pain, paralyzing indecision, and so forth. The stimulus barriers commonly exclude materials from consciousness in immediate, undiscriminating, and global fashions. The stimulus barriers do not analyze which parts of a traumatic experience are innocuous and which are paralyzing. Reasoning metonymously, they exclude the whole of the memory; by reifying associated metaphors, they add to the traumatic memory whatever closely resembles it. Because the ego's stimulus barriers do not distinguish among the psychic materials that they censor, they are inexact and wasteful. They exclude much that is potentially tolerable to consciousness. At the same time, they prevent consciousness from discerning how injudicious any given exercise of censorship has been. The unconscious thoughts are not available for conscious inspection. The ego's conscious decision-making process cannot retrospectively evaluate the extent to which an act of censorship was necessary or, once instituted, remains necessary or wise.

Metaphoric thinking serves the psyche, among other manners, as a feedback loop that returns to consciousness as much excluded material as consciousness can tolerate. The recycling process is accomplished through displacement and the return of the repressed. The repressed returns because the dream-work takes secondary process ideas that are current, associates them with secondary process materials that are presently being barred from consciousness, translates the several ideas into forms that are able to communicate with the instinctual desires of the primary process, submits the associations to imaginative problem-solving, and returns the wealth of materials to consciousness. Much that would otherwise be lost to consciousness is thereby restored.

The ego's stimulus barriers ordinarily limit the return of the repressed by resisting insight into the displacements. As long as a displacement's latent contents are repressed, its metaphoric meaning fails to be reconstructed by consciousness.

Because insight can be therapeutic without being complete, it is possible for consciousness to gain a partial insight into a displacement without recognizing the symbol as a metaphor. As a clinical technique, the provision of partial insight has been termed "interpretation within the metaphor" (Ekstein & Wallerstein, 1956; Cain & Maupin, 1961; Aleksandrowicz, 1962; Caruth & Ekstein, 1966). Partial insight may also be considered normative achievements of play, art, folklore, and religion. Consider Freud's (1920, pp. 14–17) account of the abreactive function of play. Analyzing the play of an infant nephew, Freud suggested that his game of *fort-da* replicated a situation that had been distressing in reality. Where the boy had been passive during the real experience, he took an active role within the play situation. The game was an effort "to work over in the mind some overpowering experience so as to make oneself master of it" (p. 16). Freud attributed the same function to "the artistic play and artistic imagination carried out by adults" (p. 17). I would suggest a general rule. Not only does symbol formation reclaim nontraumatic materials whose censorship is unnecessary, but displacements of distressing or traumatic materials are attempted solutions of the conflicts. Like the healthy inflammation of a wound, they are part of the healing process, not part of the wound.

Summary

Freud's discussion of the primary process of generating perceptual identities and the secondary process of formulating thought identities belongs in the classic tradition of Aristotlean psychology. It can also be understood in semiotic terms. The id depends on mental elements that are psychological analogs of synecdoches; the ego on metonyms.

Metaphoric thinking may be attributed to the superego on the basis of the occasional occurrence of metaphors in the manifest content of dreams. On theoretic grounds, we may recognize every dream symbol as a metaphor that is not known as such during dreaming, and every creative inspiration as a metaphor that relational thinking may or may not develop into an analog, model, or other heurism. Metaphor is the *conditio sine qua non* of abstract thinking, fictional or imaginative thinking, language, and the return of the repressed. The superego's interpersonal functions may be treated as applications of metaphoric thinking to the inborn task of representing the perspective of the object.

Works Cited

Abell, Arthur M. (1955). *Talks with Great Composers*. New York: Philosophical Library.

Abraham, Karl. (1924). A short study of the development of the libido, viewed in the light of mental disorders. In: *Selected Papers of Karl Abraham*, trans. Douglas Bryan & Alix Strachey. 1927; reprinted New York: Brunner/Mazel, n.d., pp. 418–501.

Adler, Alfred. (1936). On the interpretation of dreams. *International Journal of Individual Psychology* 2:3–16.

Alexander, Franz. (1925). A metapsychological description of the process of cure. In: *The Scope of Psychoanalysis 1921–1961: Selected Papers of Franz Alexander*. New York: Basic Books, pp. 205–24.

———. (1929). *The Psychoanalysis of the Total Personality: The Application of Freud's Theory of the Ego to the Neuroses*, trans. Bernard Glueck & Bertram D. Lewin. Reprinted New York & Washington: Nervous and Mental Disease Publishing, 1935.

———. (1948). *Fundamentals of Psychoanalysis*. New York: W. W. Norton.

Aleksandrowicz, Dov R. (1962). The meaning of metaphor. *Bulletin of the Menninger Clinic* 26:92–101.

Arieti, Silvano. (1976). *Creativity: The Magic Synthesis*. New York: Basic Books.

Aristotle. (1984). On the soul. In: *The Complete Works of Aristotle: The Revised Oxford Translation*, ed. Jonathan Barnes. Princeton: Princeton University Press, Vol. II, pp. 641–92.

Arlow, Jacob A. (1969). Unconscious fantasy and disturbances of conscious experience. *Psychoanalytic Quarterly* 38:1–27.

———. (1979). Metaphor and the psychoanalytic situation. *Psychoanalytic Quarterly* 48:363–85.

———. (1982). Problems of the superego concept. In: *Psychoanalysis: Clinical Theory and Practice.* Madison, CT: International Universities Press, pp. 367–79.

———. (1989). Psychoanalysis and the quest for morality. In: Harold P. Blum, Edward M. Weinshel, & F. Robert Rodman (Eds.), *The Psychoanalytic Core: Essays in Honor of Leo Rangell, M.D.* Madison, CT: International Universities Press, pp. 147–66.

Arlow, Jacob A. & Brenner, Charles. (1964). *Psychoanalytic Concepts and the Structural Hypothesis.* New York: International Universities Press.

Baars, Bernard J. & McGovern, Katharine. (1996). Cognitive views of consciousness. What are the facts? How can we explain them? In: Max Velmans (Ed.), *The Science of Consciousness: Psychological, Neuropsychological and Clinical Reviews.* London & New York: Routledge.

Balint, Enid. (1993). *Before I Was I: Psychoanalysis and the Imagination,* ed. Juliet Michell & Michael Parsons. London: Free Association; New York: Guilford.

Balint, Michael. (1937). Early developmental states of the ego. Primary object-love. *International Journal of Psycho-Analysis* 20 (1939): 265–73. Reprinted in: *Primary Love and Psycho-analytic Technique,* 2nd ed., pp. 74–90. London: Tavistock Publications, 1965.

Barbour, Ian G. (1974). *Myths, Models, and Paradigms: A Comparative Study in Science and Religion.* New York: Harper & Row.

Basch, Michael Franz. (1983). Empathic understanding: A review of the concept and some theoretical considerations. *Journal of the American Psychoanalytic Association* 31:101–26.

Baudry, Francis. (1974). Remarks on spoken words in the dream. *Psychoanalytic Quarterly* 43:581–605.

Bellak, Leopold. (1958). Creativity: Some random notes to a systematic consideration. *Journal of Projective Techniques* 22:363–80.

Beres, David. (1958). Vicissitudes of superego functions and superego precursors in childhood. *Psychoanalytic Study of the Child* 13:324–51.

————. (1968). The role of empathy in psychotherapy and psychoanalysis. *Journal of the Hillside Hospital* 17:362–69.

Beres, David & Arlow, Jacob. (1974). Fantasy and identification in empathy. *Psychoanalytic Quarterly* 43:26–50.

Bergler, Edmund. (1948). *The Battle of the Conscience: A Psychiatric Study of the Inner Workings of the Conscience.* Washington, DC: Washington Institute of Medicine.

————. (1949). *The Basic Neurosis: Oral Regression and Psychic Masochism.* New York: Grune & Stratton, Inc.

————. (1952). *The Superego: Unconscious Conscience—The Key to the Theory and Therapy of Neurosis.* New York: Grune & Stratton.

————. (1959). *Principles of Self-Damage.* New York: Philosophical Library; reprinted Madison, CT: International Universities Press, 1992.

Bergler, Edmund & Róheim, Géza. (1946). Psychology of time perception. *Psychoanalytic Quarterly* 15:190–207.

Bergmann, Martin S. (1971). Psychoanalytic observations on the capacity to love. In: John B. McDevitt & Calvin F. Settlage (Eds.), *Separation-Individuation: Essays in Honor of Margaret S. Mahler.* New York: International Universities Press, pp. 15–40.

Berlin, I. N. (1960). Aspects of creativity and the learning process. *American Imago* 17:83–99.

Bibring, Edward. (1937). Symposium on the theory of the therapeutic results of psycho-analysis. *International Journal of Psycho-Analysis* 18/2–3:170–89.

Bion, Wilfred R. (1962a). *Learning from Experience.* New York: Basic Books.

————. (1962b). A theory of thinking. *International Journal of Psycho-Analysis* 43:306–310. Reprinted in: *Second Thoughts: Selected Papers on Psycho-Analysis.* New York: Jason Aronson, 1967, pp. 110–19.

Bland, Kalman P., ed. & trans. (1982). *The Epistle on the Possibility of Conjunction with the Active Intellect by Ibn Rushd with the Commentary of Moses Narboni: A Critical Edition and Annotated Translation.* New York: Jewish Theological Seminary of America.

Blumenthal, David R. (1977). Maimonides' intellectualist mysticism and the superiority of the prophecy of Moses. *Studies in Medieval Culture*

10:51–68; reprinted in: David R. Blumenthal (Ed.), *Approaches to Judaism in Medieval Times*. Chico, CA: Scholars Press, 1984.

Boesky, Dale. (1983). The problem of mental representation in self and object theory. *Psychoanalytic Quarterly* 52:564–83.

Bonaparte, Marie. (1947). A lion hunter's dreams. *Psychoanalytic Quarterly* 16:1–10.

Boorstein, Sylvia. (1997). On mindfulness. In: Avram Davis (Ed.), *Meditation from the Heart of Judaism: Today's Teachers Share Their Practices, Techniques, and Faith*. Woodstock, VT: Jewish Lights Publishing, 1997, pp. 115–20.

Borbely, Antal F. (1998). A psychoanalytic concept of metaphor. *International Journal of Psycho-Analysis* 79:923–36.

Bråten, Stein. (1988). Dialogic mind: The infant and the adult in protoconversation. In: Marc E. Carvallo (Ed.), *Nature, Cognition and System*. Dordrecht, Boston & London: Kluwer Academic Publishers. Volume 1, pp. 187–205.

Breen, Hal J. (1986). A psychoanalytic approach to ethics. *Journal of the American Academy of Psychoanalysis* 14/2:255–75.

Breger, Louis. (1969). Dream function: An information processing model. In: Louis Breger (Ed.), *Clinical-Cognitive Psychology: Models and Integrations*. Englewood Cliffs, NJ: Prentice-Hall, pp. 182–227.

Brenner, Charles. (1973). *An Elementary Textbook of Psychoanalysis*, 2nd ed. New York: International Universities Press.

Brentano, F. (1867). *The Psychology of Aristotle: In Particular His Doctrine of the Active Intellect*. Trans. R. George. Berkeley: University of California Press, 1977.

Breznitz, Shlomo. (1971). A critical note on secondary revision. *International Journal of Psycho-Analysis* 52:407–12.

Brown, Daniel P. & Jack Engler. (1984). An outcome study of intensive mindfulness meditation. *Psychoanalytic Study of Society* 10:163–225.

Buie, Dan H. (1981). Empathy: Its nature and limitations. *Journal of the American Psychoanalytic Association* 29:281–307.

Burnshaw, S. (1970). *The Seamless Web*. New York: George Braziller.

Burrow, Trigant. (1914). Character and the neuroses. *Psychoanalytic Review* 1(2):121–28.

Bush, Marshall. (1969). Psychoanalysis and scientific creativity: With special reference to regression in the service of the ego. *Journal of the American Psychoanalytic Association* 17:136–90.

Cain, Albert C. & Maupin, Barbara M. (1961). Interpretation within the metaphor. *Bulletin of the Menninger Clinic* 25:307–11.

Calef, Victor (1972). A theoretical note on the ego in the therapeutic process. In: Seymour C. Post (Ed.), *Moral Values and the Superego Concept in Psychoanalysis*. New York: International Universities Press, pp. 144–66.

Cartwright, Rosalind Dymond. (1969). Dreams as compared to other forms of fantasy. In: Milton Kramer, with Roy M. Whitman, Bill J. Baldridge, & Paul H. Ornstein (Eds.), *Dream Psychology and the New Biology of Dreaming*. Springfield, IL: Charles C. Thomas, pp. 361–72.

———. (1977). *Night Life: Explorations in Dreaming*. Englewood Cliffs, NJ: Prentice-Hall.

———. (1986). Affect and dream work from an information processing point of view. *Journal of Mind and Behavior* 7:411–28.

Cartwright, Rosalind Dymond. (1969). Dreams as compared to other forms of fantasy. In *Dream Psychology and the New Biology of Dreaming*. Ed. Milton Kramer, with Roy M. Whitman, Bill J. Baldridge, & Paul H. Ornstein. Springfield, IL: Charles C. Thomas, pp. 361–72.

———. (1986). Affect and dream work from an information processing point of view. *Journal of Mind and Behavior* 7:411–28.

Caruth, Elaine & Ekstein, Rudolf. (1966). Interpretation within the metaphor: Further considerations. *Journal of the American Academy of Child Psychiatry* 5:35–46.

Casey, Robert P. (1943). Dreams and decision. *Psychiatry* 6:71–73.

Chasseguet-Smirgel, Janine. (1976). Some thoughts on the ego ideal: A contribution to the study of the 'illness of ideality.' *Psychoanalytic Quarterly* 45:344–73.

———. (1985). *The Ego Ideal: A Psychoanalytic Essay on the Malady of the Ideal*, trans. Paul Barrows. New York: W. W. Norton.

Cohn, Ruth C. (1968). Training intuition. In: Herbert Otto & John Mann (Eds.), *Ways of Growth*. New York: Grossman Publishers.

Dement, William C. (1964). Experimental dream studies. In: Jules H. Masserman (Ed.), *Science and Psychoanalysis, Volume VII: Development and Research*. New York: Grune & Stratton, pp. 129–62.

Deri, Susan K. (1984). *Symbolization and Creativity.* New York: International Universities Press.

Deutsch, Felix. (1959). Creative passion of the artist and its synesthetic aspects. *International Journal of Psycho-Analysis* 40:38–51.

Deutsch, Francine & Madle, Ronald A. (1975). Empathy: Historic and current conceptualizations, measurement, and a cognitive theoretical perspective. *Human Development* 18:267–87.

Dewan, Edmond M. (1970). The programing (P) hypothesis for REM sleep. In: Ernest Hartmann (Ed.), *Sleep and Dreaming.* Boston: Little, Brown, pp. 295–307.

Dooley, Lucile. (1941). The concept of time in defence of ego integrity. *Psychiatry* 4:13–23.

Dorpat, Theo L. (1981). Basic concepts and terms in object relations theory. In: Saul Tuttman, Carol Kaye, & Muriel Zimmerman (Eds.), *Object and Self: A Developmental Approach. Essays in Honor of Edith Jacobson.* New York: International Universities Press.

Eagle, Morris N. (1981). Interests as object relations. *Psychoanalysis and Contemporary Thought* 4:527–65.

Edelheit, Henry. (1968). Language and the development of the ego. *Journal of the American Psychoanalytic Association* 16:113–22.

Ehrenzweig, Anton. (1948–49). Unconscious form-creation in art. *British Journal of Medical Psychology* 21:185–214; 22:88–109.

———. (1953). *The Psychoanalysis of Artistic Vision and Hearing: An Introduction to a Theory of Unconscious Perception.* London: Routledge & Kegan Paul; reprinted London: Sheldon Press, 1975.

———. (1964). The undifferentiated matrix of artistic imagination. *Psychoanalytic Study of Society* 3:373–98.

———. (1967). *The Hidden Order of Art.* Berkeley: University of California Press.

Ekstein, Rudolf & Wallerstein, Judith. (1956). Observations on the psychotherapy of borderline and psychotic children. *Psychoanalytic Study of the Child* 11:303–11.

Emde, Robert N. (1988). Development terminable and interminable. I. Innate and motivational factors from infancy. *International Journal of Psycho-Analysis* 69:23–42.

Ephron, Harmon S. & Carrington, Patricia. (1967). Ego functioning in rapid eye movement sleep: Implications for dream theory. In: Jules H. Masserman (Ed.), *Science and Psychoanalysis, Volume XI: The Ego*. New York: Grune & Stratton, pp. 75–94.

Epstein, Mark. (1988). The deconstruction of the self: Ego and "egolessness" in Buddhist insight meditation. *Journal of Transpersonal Psychology* 20(1):61–69.

Erikson, Erik Homburger. (1954). The dream specimen of psychoanalysis. *Journal of the American Psychoanalytic Association* 2:5–56.

———. (1958). *Young Man Luther*. New York: W. W. Norton.

———. (1977). *Toys and Reasons: Stages in the Ritualization of Experience*. New York: W. W. Norton.

Eyre, Dean P. (1978). Identification and empathy. *International Review of Psycho-Analysis* 5:351–59.

Fairbairn, W. Ronald D. (1941). A revised psychopathology of the psychoses and psychoneuroses. Reprinted in: *Psychoanalytic Studies of the Personality*, 1952; reprinted London & New York: Tavistock/Routledge, 1990, pp. 28–58.

———. (1943). The repression and the return of bad objects (with special reference to the 'war neuroses'). Reprinted in: *Psychoanalytic Studies of the Personality*, pp. 59–81.

———. (1963). Synopsis of an object-relations theory of the personality. *International Journal of Psycho-Analysis* 44:224–25.

Fakhry, Majid. (1971). Three varieties of mysticism in Islam. *International Journal for the Philosophy of Religion* 2(4):193–207.

Fenichel, Otto. (1928). The clinical aspect of the need for punishment. *International Journal of Psycho-Analysis* 9:47–70.

———. (1945). *The Psychoanalytic Theory of Neurosis*. New York: W. W. Norton.

Ferenczi, Sandor. (1928). The elasticity of psycho-analytic technique. *International Zeitschrift für Psychoanalyse* 14:197f. In: *Final Contributions to the Problems and Methods of Psycho-Analysis*, trans. Eric Mosbacher and others. London: Hogarth Press, 1955; reprinted New York: Brunner/Mazel, 1980, pp. 87–107.

Ferreira, Antonio J. (1961). Empathy and the bridge function of the ego. *Journal of the American Psychoanalytic Association* 9:91–105.

Fiss, Harry, Klein, George S., & Shollar, Edward. (1974). "Dream intensification" as a function of prolonged REM-period interruption. *Psychoanalysis and Contemporary Science* 3:399–424.

Fliess, Robert. (1942). The metapsychology of the analyst. *Psychoanalytic Quarterly* 11:211–27.

———. (1973). *Symbol, Dream, and Psychosis.* New York: International Universities Press.

Flugel, J. C. (1945). *Man, Morals and Society: A Psych-analytical Study.* Reprinted New York: International Universities Press, 1970.

Forisha, Barbara L. (1981). Patterns of creativity and mental imagery in men and women. *Journal of Mental Imagery* 5:85–96.

Fosshage, James L. (1983). The psychological function of dreams: A revised psychoanalytic perspective. *Psychoanalysis and Contemporary Thought* 6/4:641–69.

———. (1987). New vistas in dream interpretation. In: Myron L. Glucksman & Silas L. Warner (Eds.), *Dreams in New Perspective: The Royal Road Revisited.* New York: Human Sciences Press, pp. 23–43.

Freemantle, Anne (Ed.), (1964). *The Protestant Mystics.* New York: New American Library, 1965.

French, Thomas Morton. (1937a). Reality and the unconscious. *Psychoanalytic Quarterly* 6:23–61.

———. (1937b). Reality testing in dreams. *Psychoanalytic Quarterly* 6:62–77.

———. (1938). Defense and synthesis in the function of the ego. *Psychoanalytic Quarterly* 7:537–53. Reprinted in: *Psychoanalytic Interpretations: The Selected Papers of Thomas M. French, M.D.* Chicago: Quadrangle, 1970, pp. 134–47.

———. (1939). Insight and distortion in dreams. In: *Psychoanalytic Interpretations,* pp. 107–19.

———. (1952). *The Integration of Behavior. Vol. I—Basic Postulates.* Chicago: University of Chicago Press.

———. (1954). *The Integration of Behavior. Vol. II—The Integrative Process in Dreams.* Chicago: University of Chicago Press.

———. (1957). Analysis of the dream censorship. In: George E. Daniels, James P. Cattell, Williard M. Gaylin, Terry C. Rodgers, & Daniel Shapiro (Eds.), *New Perspectives in Psychoanalysis: Sandor Rado*

Lectures 1957–1963. New York: Grune & Stratton, 1965, pp. 1–19. Reprinted in: *Psychoanalytic Interpretations*, pp. 240–57.

———. (1970). Guilt, shame, and other reactive motives. In: *Psychoanalytic Interpretations*, pp. 258–68. Chicago: Quadrangle Books.

French, Thomas M. & Fromm, Erika. (1964). *Dream Interpretation: A New Approach.* New York: Basic Books.

French, Thomas & Whitman, Roy M. (1969). A focal conflict view. In: Milton Kramer, with Roy M. Whitman, Bill J. Baldridge, & Paul H. Ornstein (Eds.), *Dream Psychology and the New Biology of Dreaming.* Springfield, IL: Charles C. Thomas, pp. 65–77.

Freud, Anna. (1927). Four lectures on child analysis. Reprinted in: *Introduction to Psychoanalysis: Lectures for Child Analysts and Teachers 1922–1935.* London: Hogarth Press, 1974, pp. 1–69.

———. ([1936] 1966). *The Ego and the Mechanisms of Defense*, 2nd ed. New York: International Universities Press, 1980.

Freud, Sigmund. All references are to *The Standard Edition of the Complete Psychological Works of Sigmund Freud*, 24 vols, ed. James Strachey. London: Hogarth Press.

———. (1900). The interpretation of dreams. *Standard Edition*, 4–5:1–625. London: Hogarth Press, 1958.

———. (1901a). On dreams. *Standard Edition*, 5:633–86. London: Hogarth Press, 1958.

———. (1901b). The psychopathology of everyday life. *Standard Edition*, 6:1–279. London: Hogarth Press, 1960.

———. (1905a). Fragment of an analysis of a case of hysteria. *Standard Edition*, 7:7–122. London: Hogarth Press, 1953.

———. (1905b). Three essays on the theory of sexuality. *Standard Edition*, 7:130–243. London: Hogarth Press, 1953.

———. (1908a). Creative writers and day-dreaming. *Standard Edition*, 9:143–53. London: Hogarth Press, 1959.

———. (1908b). Hysterical phantasies and their relation to bisexuality. *Standard Edition*, 9:159–66. London: Hogarth Press, 1959.

———. (1910). Five lectures on psycho-analysis. *Standard Edition*, 11:9–55. London: Hogarth Press, 1957.

————. (1911). Formulations on the two principles of mental functioning. *Standard Edition*, 12:218–26. London: Hogarth Press, 1958.

————. (1913). Totem and taboo: Some points of agreement between the mental life of savages and neurotics. *Standard Edition*, 13:1–161. London: Hogarth Press, 1958.

————. (1914). On narcissism: an introduction. *Standard Edition*, 14:78–102. London: Hogarth Press, 1957.

————. (1915b). Repression. *Standard Edition*, 14:146–58. London: Hogarth Press, 1957.

————. (1915c). The unconscious. *Standard Edition*, 14:166–204. London: Hogarth Press, 1957.

————. (1916–17). Introductory lectures on psycho-analysis. *Standard Edition*, 15–16:9–463. London: Hogarth Press, 1961–63.

————. (1917). Mourning and melancholia. *Standard Edition*, 14:243–58. London: Hogarth Press, 1957.

————. (1920). Beyond the pleasure principle. *Standard Edition*, 18:7–64. London: Hogarth Press, 1955.

————. (1921). Group psychology and the analysis of the ego. *Standard Edition*, 18:69–143. London: Hogarth Press, 1955.

————. (1923a). The ego and the id. *Standard Edition*, 19:12–59. London: Hogarth Press, 1961.

————. (1923b). Joseph Popper-Lynkeus and the theory of dreams. *Standard Edition*, 19:261–63. London: Hogarth Press, 1961.

————. (1923c). Remarks on the theory and practice of dream interpretation. *Standard Edition*, 19:109–21. London: Hogarth Press, 1961.

————. (1923d). Two encyclopedia articles. *Standard Edition*, 18:235–59. London: Hogarth Press, 1955.

————. (1924). The dissolution of the Oedipus complex. *Standard Edition*, 19:173–79. London: Hogarth Press, 1961.

————. (1925a). Negation. *Standard Edition*, 19:235–39. London: Hogarth Press, 1961.

————. (1925b). Some additional notes on dream-interpretation as a whole. *Standard Edition*, 19:127–38. London: Hogarth Press, 1961.

————. (1925c). Some psychical consequences of the anatomical distinction between the sexes. *Standard Edition*, 19:248–63. London: Hogarth Press, 1961.

———. (1926). Inhibitions, symptoms, and anxiety. *Standard Edition*, 20:87–172. London: Hogarth Press, 1959.

———. (1927a). The future of an illusion. *Standard Edition*, 21:5–56. London: Hogarth Press, 1961.

———. (1927b). Humour. *Standard Edition*, 21:151–66. London: Hogarth Press, 1961.

———. (1928). Dostoevsky and parricide. *Standard Edition*, 21:177–94. London: Hogarth Press, 1961.

———. (1930). Civilization and its discontents. *Standard Edition*, 21:64–145. London: Hogarth Press, 1961.

———. (1933). New introductory lectures on psycho-analysis. *Standard Edition*, 22:5–182. London: Hogarth Press, 1964.

———. (1940). An outline of psycho-analysis. *Standard Edition*, 23:144–207. London: Hogarth Press, 1964.

Fromm, Erich. (1947). *Man for Himself: An Inquiry into the Psychology of Ethics*. Holt, Rinehart & Winston; reprinted Greenwich, CT: Fawcett, n.d.

Fromm, Erika & French, Thomas M. (1962). Formation and evaluation of hypotheses in dream interpretation. *Journal of Psychology* 54:271–83.

Furer, Manuel. (1967). Some developmental aspects of the superego. *International Journal of Psycho-Analysis* 48:277–80.

———. (1972). The history of the superego concept in psychoanalysis: A review of the literature. In: Seymour C. Post (Ed.), *Moral Values and the Superego Concept in Psychoanalysis*. New York: International Universities Press, pp. 11–62.

Gaddini, Eugenio. (1969). On imitation. *International Journal of Psycho-Analysis* 50:475–84. Reprinted in: *A Psychoanalytic Theory of Infantile Experience: Conceptual and Clinical Reflections*. London & New York: Tavistock/Routledge, 1992, pp. 18–34.

Garma, Angel. (1946). The traumatic situation in the genesis of dreams. *International Journal of Psycho-Analysis* 27:134–39.

Gay, Volney Patrick. (1992). *Freud on Sublimation: Reconsiderations*. Albany: State University of New York Press.

Gedo, John E. (1972). On the psychology of genius. *International Journal of Psycho-Analysis* 53:199–203.

————. (1979). The psychology of genius revisited. *Annual of Psychoanalysis* 7:269–83.

Gibson, J. J. (1979). *The Ecological Approach to Visual Perception*. Boston: Houghton-Mifflin.

Glenn, Jules. (1974). Twins in disguise: A psychoanalytic essay on sleuth and the royal hunt of the sun. *Psychoanalytic Quarterly* 43:288–302.

————. (1989). Synthetic and conflictual aspects of the superego: A case study. In: Harold P. Blum, Edward M. Weinshel, & F. Robert Rodman (Eds.), *The Psychoanalytic Core: Essays in Honor of Leo Rangell, M.D.* Madison, CT: International Universities Press, pp. 225–41.

Glover, Edward. (1937). Symposium on the theory of the therapeutic results of psycho-analysis. *International Journal of Psycho-Analysis* 18:125–33.

Goodman, Stanley (reporter). (1965). Current status of the theory of the superego. *Journal of the American Psychoanalytic Association* 13:172–80.

Greenacre, Phyllis. (1956). Re-evaluation of the process of working through. *International Journal of Psycho-Analysis* 37:439–44.

————. (1957). The childhood of the artist. *Psychoanalytic Study of the Child* 12:47–72.

————. (1958). The family romance of the artist. *Psychoanalytic Study of the Child* 13:9–43.

————. (1960). Woman as artist. *Psychoanalytic Quarterly* 29:208–27.

Greenberg, Ramon. (1981). Dreams and REM sleep—An integrative approach. In: William Fishbein (Ed.), *Sleep, Dreams and Memory*. New York: SP Medical & Scientific Books, pp. 125–33.

————. (1987). The dream problem and problems in dreams. In: Myron L. Glucksman & Silas L. Warner (Eds.), *Dreams in New Perspective: The Royal Road Revisited*. New York: Human Sciences Press, pp. 45–57.

Greenberg, Ramon, Katz, Howard, Schwartz, Wynn, & Pearlman, Chester. (1992). A research-based reconsideration of the psychoanalytic theory of dreaming. *Journal of the American Psychoanalytic Association* 40:531–50.

Greenberg, Ramon & Pearlman, Chester. (1975). A psychoanalytic-dream continuum: The source and function of dreams. *International Review of Psycho-Analysis* 2:441–48.

———. (1978). If Freud only knew: A reconsideration of psychoanalytic dream theory. *International Review of Psycho-Analysis* 5:71–75.

Greenberg, Ramon, Pearlman, Chester A., & Gampel, Dorothy. (1972). War neuroses and the adaptive function of REM sleep. *British Journal of Medical Psychology* 45:27–33.

Greenberg, Ramon, Pillard, Richard, & Pearlman, Chester. (1972). The effect of dream (stage REM) deprivation on adaptation to stress. *Psychosomatic Medicine* 34(3):257–62.

Greenson, Ralph R. (1954). The struggle against identification. *Journal of the American Psychoanalytic Association* 2:200–17.

———. (1960). Empathy and its vicissitudes. *International Journal of Psycho-Analysis* 41:418–24.

———. (1967). *The Technique and Practice of Psychoanalysis*, Vol. 1. New York: International Universities Press.

Grossman, William I. (1982). The self as fantasy: Fantasy as theory. *Journal of the American Psychoanalytic Association* 30(4):919–37.

———. (1992). Hierarchies, boundaries, and representation in a Freudian model of mental organization. *Journal of the American Psychoanalytic Association* 40:27–62.

Hardy, Sir Alister. (1979). *The Spiritual Nature of Man: A Study of Contemporary Religious Experience*. Oxford: Clarendon Press.

Harrison, Irving B. (1986). On "merging" and the fantasy of merging. *Psychoanalytic Study of the Child* 41:155–70.

Hartmann, Ernest L. (1973). *The Functions of Sleep*. New Haven: Yale University Press.

———. (1976). Discussion of "The changing use of dreams in psychoanalytic practice." *International Journal of Psycho-Analysis* 57:331–34.

Hartmann, Heinz. ([1939] 1958). *Ego Psychology and the Problem of Adaptation*. New York: International Universities Press, 1958.

———. (1960). *Psychoanalysis and Moral Values*. New York: International Universities Press.

Hartmann, Heinz, Kris, Ernst, & Loewenstein, Rudolph M. (1946). Comments on the formation of psychic structure. *Psychoanalytic Study of the Child* 2:11–38. Reprinted in: *Papers on Psychoanalytic Psychology*. (Psychological Issues, Vol. IV, No. 2, Monograph 14.) New York: International Universities Press, 1964, pp. 27–55.

Harvey, E. Ruth. (1975). *The Inward Wits: Psychological Theory in the Middle Ages and the Renaissance.* London: Warburg Institute—University of London.

Hawkins, David R. (1966). A review of psychoanalytic dream theory in the light of recent psycho-physiological studies of sleep and dreaming. *British Journal of Medical Psychology* 39:85–104.

Heschel, Abraham J. (1996). *Prophetic Inspiration after the Prophets: Maimonides and Other Medieval Authorities.* Ed. Morris Faierstein. Hoboken, NJ: Ktav.

Hesse, Mary. (1970). *Models and Analogies in Science.* Notre Dame: Notre Dame University Press, 1970.

Heynick, Frank. (1981). Linguistic aspects of Freud's dream model. *International Review of Psycho-Analysis* 8:299–314.

———. (1993). *Language and Its Disturbances in Dreams: The Pioneering Work of Freud and Kraepelin Updated.* New York: John Wiley & Sons, 1993.

Isakower, Otto. (1954). Spoken words in dreams: A preliminary communication. *Psychoanalytic Quarterly* 23:1–6.

Jacobson, Edith. (1954a). Contribution to the metapsychology of psychotic identifications. *Journal of the American Psychoanalytic Association* 2:239–62.

———. (1954b). The self and the object world: Vicissitudes of their infantile cathexes and their influence on ideational and affective development. *Psychoanalytic Study of the Child* 9:75–127.

———. (1964). *The Self and The Object World.* New York: International Universities Press.

Jakobson, Roman. (1956). Two aspects of language and two types of aphasic disturbances. *Fundamentals of Language.* The Hague: Mouton. Reprinted in: *Selected Writings, Volume II: Word and Language.* The Hague: Mouton, 1971.

James, William. (1902). *The Varieties of Religious Experience: A Study in Human Nature.* New York: New American Library, 1958.

Jekels, Ludwig & Bergler, Edmund. ([1934] 1949). Transference and love. [*Imago* 20:5–31] Trans. Henry Alden Bunker. *Psychoanalytic Quarterly* 18/3. Reprinted in: Ludwig Jekels. *Selected Papers.* New York: International Universities Press, 1952, pp. 178–201.

———. (1940). Instinct dualism in dreams. *Psychoanalytic Quarterly* 9:394–414.

Jones, Ernest. (1928). Psycho-analysis and folklore. Reprinted in: *Psycho-Myth, Psycho-History*, Vol. II, pp. 1–21.

Jones, Richard M. (1962). *Ego Synthesis in Dreams*. Cambridge, MA: Schenkman.

———. (1965). Dream interpretation and the psychology of dreaming. *Journal of the American Psychoanalytic Association* 13:304–19.

———. (1969). An epigenetic analysis of dreams. In: Milton Kramer, with Roy M. Whitman, Bill J. Baldridge, & Paul H. Ornstein (Eds.), *Dream Psychology and the New Biology of Dreaming*. Springfield, IL: Charles C. Thomas, pp. 265–76.

———. (1970a). *The New Psychology of Dreaming*. New York: Grune & Stratton.

———. (1970b). The transformation of the stuff dreams are made of. In: Ernest Hartmann (Ed.), *Sleep and Dreaming*. Boston: Little, Brown, pp. 221–27.

Jung, Carl Gustav. (1938). *Psychology and Religion*. New Haven: Yale University Press.

Keiser, Sylvan. (1962). Disturbance of ego functions of speech and abstract thinking. *Journal of the American Psychoanalytic Association* 10:50–73.

Kelman, Harvey. (1975). The 'day precipitate' of dreams: The Morris hypothesis. *International Journal of Psycho-Analysis* 56:209–18.

Kernberg, Otto F. (1966). Structural derivatives of object relationships. *International Journal of Psycho-Analysis* 47:236–53. Reprinted in: *Object-Relations Theory and Clinical Psychoanalysis*. Northvale, NJ: Jason Aronson, 1990.

———. (1975). *Borderline Conditions and Pathological Narcissism*. Northvale, NJ: Jason Aronson, 1990.

———. (1976). *Object-Relations Theory and Clinical Psychoanalysis*. Northvale, NJ: Jason Aronson, 1990.

———. (1980). *Internal World and External Reality: Object Relations Theory Applied*. New York: Jason Aronson.

———. (1984). *Severe Personality Disorders: Psychotherapeutic Strategies*. New Haven: Yale University Press.

————. (1993). The couple's constructive and destructive superego functions. *Journal of the American Psychoanalytic Association* 41(3):653–77.

Kirk, Russell. (1971). *Eliot and His Age*. New York: Random House.

Klein, George S. (1962). On inhibition, disinhibition, and "primary process" in thinking. In: G. Nielson (Ed.), *Proceedings of the XIV International Congress of Applied Psychology*, Vol. 4, *Clinical Psychology*. Copenhagen: Munksgaard, pp. 179–98.

Klein, Melanie. (1929). Personification in the play of children. Reprinted in: *Love, Guilt and Reparation: and Other Works 1921–1945*. New York: Delacourt Press, 1975, pp. 199–209.

————. (1932). *The Psycho-Analysis of Children*, trans. Alix Strachey, with H. A. Thorner. New York: Delacorte Press, 1975.

————. (1948). On the theory of anxiety and guilt. Reprinted in: *Envy and Gratitude: and Other Works 1946–1963*. New York: Free Press, 1975, pp. 25–42.

————. (1952). On observing the behaviour of young infants. Reprinted in: *Envy and Gratitude*, pp. 94–121.

Kligerman, Charles (reporter). (1972). Panel on 'Creativity.' *International Journal of Psycho-Analysis* 53:21–30.

Koestler, Arthur. (1964). *The Act of Creation*. London: Hutchinson.

Kohut, Heinz. (1959). Introspection, empathy, and psychoanalysis: An examination of the relationship between mode of observation and theory. In: *The Search for the Self: Selected Writings of Heinz Kohut: 1950–1978*, ed. Paul H. Ornstein. New York: International Universities Press, 1978, Vol. 1, pp. 205–32.

————. (1971). *The Analysis of the Self: A Systematic Approach to the Psychoanalytic Treatment of Narcissistic Personality Disorders*. Madison, CT: International Universities Press.

————. (1977). *The Restoration of the Self*. New York: International Universities Press.

————. (1981a). Introspection, empathy, and the semicircle of mental health. In: *The Search for the Self: Selected Writings of Heinz Kohut: 1978–1981*, Vol. 4, ed. Paul H. Ornstein. Madison, CT: International Universities Press, 1991, pp. 527–67.

————. (1981b). On empathy. In: *The Search for the Self*, Vol. 4, pp. 525–35.

———. (1984). *How Does Analysis Cure?* Ed. Arnold Goldberg with Paul Stepansky. Chicago: University of Chicago Press.

Kornfield, Jack. (1977). *Living Buddhist Masters.* Unity Press; Kandy, Sri Lanka: Buddhist Publication Society, 1988.

———. (1979). Intensive insight meditation: A phenomenological study. *Journal of Transpersonal Psychology* 11(1):41–58.

Kris, Ernst. (1934). The psychology of caricature. *Imago* 20. Trans. in: *International Journal of Psycho-Analysis* 17 (1936). Reprinted in: *Psychoanalytic Exploration in Art.* New York: International Universities Press, 1952, pp. 173–88.

———. (1939). On inspiration. *International Journal of Psycho-Analysis* 20. Reprinted in: *Psychoanalytic Explorations in Art,* pp. 291–302.

———. (1950). On preconscious mental processes. *Psychoanalytic Quarterly* 19. Reprinted in: *Psychoanalytic Explorations in Art,* pp. 303–18.

Kubie, Lawrence S. (1953). The distortion of the symbolic process in neurosis and psychosis. *Journal of the American Psychoanalytic Association* 1(1):59–86.

———. (1958). *Neurotic Distortions of the Creative Process.* New York: Noonday Press.

Lacan, Jacques. (1957). The agency of the letter in the unconscious or reason since Freud. In *Écrits: A Selection.* Trans. Alan Sheridan. New York: W. W. Norton & Company, 1977, pp. 146–78.

Laing, R. D. (1967). Family and individual structure. In: P. Lomas (Ed.), *The Predicament of the Family.* New York: International Universities Press, pp. 107–25.

Lakoff, George. (1993). The contemporary theory of metaphor. In: Andrew Ortony (Ed.), *Metaphor and Thought,* Second Edition. Cambridge: University Press, pp. 202–51.

Lakoff, George & Johnson, Mark. (1980). *Metaphors We Live By.* Chicago: University of Chicago Press.

Langer, Susanne K. (1957). *Philosophy in a New Key: A Study in the Symbolism of Reason, Rite, and Art,* 3rd ed. Cambridge, MA: Harvard University Press.

Langs, Robert. (1986). Clinical issues arising from a new model of the mind. *Contemporary Psychoanalysis* 22:418–44.

———. (1987a). Clarifying a new model of the mind. *Contemporary Psychoanalysis* 23:162–80.

———. (1987b). A new model of the mind. *Yearbook for Psychoanalysis and Psychotherapy* 2:3–33.

———. (1988). *Decoding Your Dreams*. New York: Henry Holt.

———. (1991). *Take Charge of Your Emotional Life: Self-analysis Day by Day*. New York: Henry Holt.

———. (1992). *A Clinical Workbook for Psychotherapists*. London: Karnac.

———. (1994a). *Doing Supervision and Being Supervised*. London: Karnac Books.

———. (1994b). *The Dream Workbook: Simple Exercises to Unravel the Secrets of Your Dreams*. Brooklyn, NY: Alliance.

———. (1994c). *The Therapeutic Interaction: Synthesis of the Multiple Components of Therapy*. Northvale, NJ: Jason Aronson.

LaPiere, Richard. (1960). *The Freudian Ethic*. London: George Allen & Unwin.

LaPlanche, Jean & Pontalis, J.-B. (1973). *The Language of Psycho-Analysis*, trans. Donald Nicholson-Smith. New York: W. W. Norton.

Leary, David E. (Ed.), (1990). *Metaphors in the History of Psychology*. Cambridge: Cambridge University Press.

Leatherdale, W. H. (1974). *The Role of Analogy, Model, and Metaphor in Science*. Amsterdam: North-Holland, & New York: American Elsevier.

Leavitt, Harry C. (1957). Teleological contributions of dreams to the waking ego. *Psychoanalytic Review* 44:212–19.

Leavy, Stanley A. (1973). Psychoanalytic interpretation. *Psychoanalytic Study of the Child* 28:305–30.

Leddy, Thomas. (1995). Metaphor and metaphysics. *Metaphor and Symbolic Activity* 10(3):205–22.

Lee, Harry B. (1948). Spirituality and beauty in artistic experience. *Psychoanalytic Quarterly* 17:487–523.

———. (1949). Projective features of contemplative artistic experience. *American Journal of Orthopsychiatry* 19:101–11.

Levison, John R. (1997). *The Spirit in First Century Judaism*. Leiden: Brill.

Lewin, Bertram D. (1952). Phobic symptoms and dream interpretation. *Psychoanalytic Quarterly* 21:295–322.

———. (1958). *Dreams and the Uses of Regression*. New York: International Universities Press.

———. (1962). Knowledge and dreams. Reprinted in: *Selected Writings of Bertram D. Lewin*, ed. Jacob A. Arlow. New York: Psychoanalytic Quarterly, 1973, pp. 353–68.

Loevinger, Jane. (1976). Origins of conscience. In: Merton M. Gill & Philip S. Holzman (Eds.), *Psychology versus Metapsychology: Psychoanalytic Essays in Memory of George S. Klein*. (Psychological Issues IX/4, Monograph 36.) New York: International Universities Press, pp. 265–97.

Loewald, Hans W. (1962). Superego and time. Reprinted in: *Papers on Psychoanalysis*. New Haven: Yale University Press, 1980, pp. 43–52.

———. (1970). Psychoanalytic theory and the psychoanalytic Process. In: *Papers on Psychoanalysis*, pp. 277–301. New Haven: Yale University Press, 1980.

———. (1973). On internalization. *International Journal of Psycho-Analysis* 54:9–17.

———. (1978). Primary process, secondary process, and language. In: Joseph H. Smith (Eds.), *Psychiatry and the Humanities, Volume III: Psychoanalysis and Language*. New Haven: Yale University Press. Reprinted in: *Papers on Psychoanalysis*, pp. 178–206.

———. (1979). The waning of the Oedipus complex. *Journal of the American Psychoanalytic Association* 27. Reprinted in: *Papers on Psychoanalysis*. New Haven: Yale University Press, 1980, pp. 384–404.

———. (1980). *Papers on Psychoanalysis*. New Haven: Yale University Press.

Loewenstein, Rudolph M. (1949). A posttraumatic dream. *Psychoanalytic Quarterly* 18:449–53.

———. (1963). Some considerations on free association. *Journal of the American Psychoanalytic Association* 11:451–73.

———. (1966). On the theory of the superego: A discussion. In: Rudolph M. Loewenstein, Lottie M. Newman, Max Schur, & Albert J. Solnit (Eds.), *Psychoanalysis—A General Psychology: Essays in Honor of Heinz Hartmann*, ed. New York: International Universities Press.

Lyons, John. (1977). *Chomsky*, 2nd ed. London: Fontana/Collins.

MacCormac, Earl R. (1976). *Metaphor and Myth in Science and Religion*. Durham: Duke University Press.

Maeder, A. E. (1916). *The Dream Problem*, trans. Frank Mead Hallock & Smith Ely Jelliffe. New York: Nervous and Mental Disease Publishing Company.

Mahon, Eugene J. (1991). The "dissolution" of the Oedipus complex: A neglected cognitive factor. *Psychoanalytic Quarterly* 60:628–34.

Margulies, Alfred. (1989). *The Empathic Imagination*. New York: W. W. Norton & Company.

Martin, Peter A. (1956). Notes on inhibition of scientific productivity. *Psychoanalytic Quarterly* 25:415–17.

Mavromatis, Andreas. (1987). *Hypnagogia: The Unique State of Consciousness between Wakefulness and Sleep*. London & New York: Routledge.

McDougall, Joyce. (1994). Creativity and sexuality. In: Arlene Kramer Richards & Arnold D. Richards (Eds.), *The Spectrum of Psychoanalysis: Essays in Honor of Martin S. Bergmann*. Madison, CT: International Universities Press.

Meissner, W. W. (1968). Dreaming as process. *International Journal of Psycho-Analysis* 49:63–79.

———. (1978). *The Paranoid Process*. New York: Jason Aronson.

———. (1980). The problem of internalization and structure formation. *International Journal of Psycho-Analysis* 61:237–48.

———. (1982). The history of the psychoanalytic movement. In: Alan M. Jacobson & Dean X. Parmelee (Eds.), *Psychoanalysis: Critical Explorations in Contemporary Theory and Practice*. New York: Brunner/Mazel.

———. (1991). *What Is Effective in Psychoanalytic Therapy: The Move from Interpretation to Relation*. Northvale, NJ: Jason Aronson Inc.

Melnick, Burton A. (1997). Metaphor and the theory of libidinal development. *International Journal of Psycho-Analysis* 78:997–1015.

Menninger, Karl. (1973). *Whatever Became of Sin?* New York: Hawthorne.

Merkur, Dan. (1984). The nature of the hypnotic state: A psychoanalytic approach. *International Review of Psycho-Analysis* 11(3):345–54.

———. (1985). The prophecies of Jeremiah. *American Imago* 42(1):1–37.

————. (1988a). Adaptive symbolism and the theory of myth: The symbolic understanding of myths in Inuit religion. *Psychoanalytic Study of Society* 13:63–94.

————. (1988b). Prophetic initiation in Israel and Judah. *Psychoanalytic Study of Society* 12:37–67.

————. (1989a). Unitive experiences and the state of trance. In: Moshe Idel & Bernard McGinn (Eds.), *Mystical Union and Monotheistic Religion: An Ecumenical Dialogue.* New York: Macmillan.

————. (1989b). The visionary practices of Jewish apocalyptists. *Psychoanalytic Study of Society* 14:119–48.

————. (1995–96). "And he trusted in Yahweh": The transformation of Abram in Gen 12–13 and 15. *Journal of Psychology and Religion* 4–5:65–88.

————. (1998). *The Ecstatic Imagination: Psychedelic Experiences and the Psychoanalysis of Self-Actualization.* Albany: State University of New York Press.

————. (1999). *Mystical Moments and Unitive Thinking.* Albany: State University of New York Press.

Merlan, Philip. (1963). *Monopsychism Mysticism Metaconsciousness: Problems of the Soul in the Neoaristotelian and Neoplatonic Tradition.* The Hague: Martinus Nijhoff.

Miller, Arthur, Isaacs, Kenneth S. & Haggard, Ernest A. (1965). On the nature of the observing function of the ego. *British Journal of Medical Psychology* 38:161–69.

Milrod, David. (1990). The ego ideal. *Psychoanalytic Study of the Child* 45:43–60.

Modell, Arnold H. (1958). The theoretical implications of hallucinatory experiences in schizophrenia. *Journal of the American Psychoanalytic Association* 6:442–80.

————. (1987). An object relations perspective. *Psychoanalytic Inquiry* 6:233–40.

Moore, Burness E. (1975). Toward a clarification of the concept of narcissism. *Psychoanalytic Study of the Child* 30:243–76.

Morrison, Andrew P. (1983). Shame, ideal self, and narcissism. *Contemporary Psychoanalysis* 19(2):295–318.

Murray, Lynne. (1991). Intersubjectivity, object relations theory, and empirical evidence from mother-infant interactions. *Infant Mental Health Journal* 12/3:219–32.

Myers, Wayne A. (1979). Imaginary companions in childhood and adult creativity. *Psychoanalytic Quarterly* 48:292–307.

———. (1983). An athletic example of the typical examination dream. *Psychoanalytic Quarterly* 52:594–98.

———. (1989). The traumatic element in the typical dream of feeling embarrassed at being naked. *Journal of the American Psychoanalytic Association 37:117–30.*

Nass, Martin L. (1975). On hearing and inspiration in the composition of music. *Psychoanalytic Quarterly* 44:431–49.

Nathanson, Donald L. (1986). The empathic wall and the ecology of affect. *Psychoanalytic Study of the Child* 41:171–87.

Nell, Renee. (1968). Guidance through dreams. In: Herbert Otto & John Mann (Eds.), *Ways of Growth*. New York: Grossman, pp. 178–88.

Nicholas, Mary. (1994). *The Mystery of Goodness: And the Positive Moral Consequences of Psychotherapy*. New York: W. W. Norton.

Niederland, William G. (1976). Psychoanalytic approaches to artistic creativity. *Psychoanalytic Quarterly* 45:185–212.

Novey, Samuel. (1958). The meaning of the concept of mental representation of objects. *Psychoanalytic Quarterly* 27:57–79.

Noy, Pinchas. (1969). A revision of the psychoanalytic theory of the primary process. *International Journal of Psycho-Analysis* 50:155–78.

———. (1972). About art and artistic talent. *International Journal of Psycho-Analysis* 53:243–49.

Nunberg, Herman. (1931). The synthetic function of the ego. *International Journal of Psycho-Analysis* 12(2):123–40.

———. ([1932] 1955). *Principles of Psychoanalysis: Their Application to the Neuroses*, trans. Madlyn Kahr & Sidney Kahr. New York: International Universities Press.

Oberndorf, C. P. (1941). Time—Its relation to reality and purpose. *Psychoanalytic Review* 28:139–55.

Ogden, Thomas H. (1990). *The Matrix of the Mind: Object Relations and the Psychoanalytic Dialogue*. Northvale, NJ: Jason Aronson.

Olden, Christine. (1953). On adult empathy with children. *Psychoanalytic Study of the Child* 8:111–21.

Olinick, Stanley L. (1969). On empathy, and regression in service of the other. *British Journal of Medical Psychology* 42:41–49.

Ortony, Andrew (Ed.), (1979). *Metaphor and Thought*. Cambridge: University Press.

Palombo, Stanley R. (1978). The adaptive function of dreams. *Psychoanalysis and Contemporary Thought* 1:433–77.

Parens, Henri. (1970). Inner sustainment: Metapsychological considerations. *Psychoanalytic Quarterly* 39:223–39.

Parkin, Alan. (1985). Narcissism: Its structures, systems and affects. *International Journal of Psycho-Analysis* 66:143–56.

Patrick, Catharine. (1935). Creative thought in poets. *Arch. Psychol.* 26(178):1–74.

———. (1937). Creative thought in artists. *Journal of Psychology* 4:35–73.

———. (1938). Scientific thought. *Journal of Psychology* 5:55–83.

Pearlman, Jr., Chester A. (1970). The adaptive function of dreaming. In: Ernest Hartmann (Ed.), *Sleep and Dreaming*. Boston: Little, Brown, pp. 329–34.

Pfister, Oskar. (1923). *Some Applications of Psycho-Analysis*. London: George Allen & Unwin.

Piaget, Jean. (1932). *The Moral Development of the Child*, trans. Marjorie Gabain. Reprinted New York: Free Press, 1965.

———. (1951). *Play, Dreams and Imitation in Childhood*, trans. C. Gattegno & F. M. Hodgson. Reprinted London: Routledge & Kegan Paul, 1972.

Pine, Fred. (1981). In the beginning: Contributions to a psychoanalytic developmental psychology. *International Review of Psycho-Analysis* 8:15–33.

———. (1986). The "symbiotic phase" in light of current infancy research. *Bulletin of the Menninger Clinic* 50(6):564–69.

———. (1990). *Drive, Ego, Object, and Self: A Synthesis for Clinical Work*. New York: BasicBooks/HarperCollins.

Post, Stephen L. (1980). Origins, elements, and functions of therapeutic empathy. *International Journal of Psycho-Analysis* 61:277–93.

Pruyser, Paul W. (1974). *Between Belief and Unbelief.* New York: Harper & Row.

Rado, Sandor. (1928). The problem of melancholia. *International Journal of Psycho-Analysis* 9:420–38.

Rahman, Fazlur. (1958). *Prophecy in Islam: Philosophy and Orthodoxy.* London: George Allen & Unwin.

Rangell, Leo. (1956). Panel report: The dream in the practice of psycho-analysis. *Journal of the American Psychoanalytic Association* 4:122–37.

———. (1963). Structural problems in intrapsychic conflict. *Psychoanalytic Study of the Child* 18:103–38. Reprinted in: *The Human Core: The Intrapsychic Base of Behavior, Volume I: Action within the Structural View.* Madison, CT: International Universities Press, 1990, pp. 209–47.

———. (1974). A psychoanalytic perspective leading currently to the syndrome of the compromise of integrity. *International Journal of Psycho-Analysis* 55:3–12.

———. (1976). Lessons from Watergate: A derivative for psychoanalysis. *Psychoanalytic Quarterly* 45:37–61.

———. (1980). *The Mind of Watergate: An Exploration of the Compromise of Integrity.* New York: W. W. Norton.

Rapaport, David. (1958). The theory of ego autonomy: A generalization. Reprinted in: *The Collected Papers of David Rapaport,* ed. Merton M. Gill. New York: BasicBooks, 1967, pp. 722–44.

Reich, Annie. (1953). Narcissistic object choice in women. Reprinted in: *Annie Reich: Psychoanalytic Contributions.* New York: International Universities Press, 1973, pp. 179–208.

Reider, Norman. (1972). Metaphor as interpretation. *International Journal of Psycho-Analysis* 53:463–69.

Rogers, Robert. (1978). *Metaphor: A Psychoanalytic View.* Berkeley: University of California Press.

Roland, Alan. (1972). Imagery and symbolic expression in dreams and art. *International Journal of Psycho-Analysis* 53:531–39.

———. (1981). Imagery and the self in artistic creativity and psychoanalytic literary criticism. *Psychoanalytic Review* 68(3):409–20.

Rose, Gilbert J. (1972). Fusion states. In: Peter L. Giovacchini (Ed.), *Tactics and Techniques in Psychoanalytic Therapy*. London: Hogarth Press, pp. 170–88.

———. (1980). *The Power of Form: A Psychoanalytic Approach to Aesthetic Form*. New York: International Universities Press.

Rothenberg, Albert. (1976a). Homospatial thinking in creativity. *Archives of General Psychiatry* 33:17–26.

———. (1976b). Janusian thinking and creativity. *Psychoanalytic Study of Society* 7:1–30.

Rothstein, Arnold. (1983). *The Structural Hypothesis: An Evolutionary Perspective*. New York: International Universities Press.

Rubenstein, Ben & Levitt, Morton. (1980–81). The creative process and the narcissistic personality disorder. *International Journal of Psycho-Analytic Psychotherapy* 8:461–82.

Rubinfine, David L. (reporter). (1959). Some theoretical aspects of early psychic functioning. *Journal of the American Psychoanalytic Association* 7:561–76.

Ruitenbeek, Hendrik M. (1965). Introduction: Neurosis and creativity. In: Hendrik M. Ruitenbeek (Ed.), *The Creative Imagination: Psychoanalysis and the Genius of Inspiration*. Chicago: Quadrangle, pp. 15–22.

Russell, D. S. (1964). *The Method and Message of Jewish Apocalyptic 200 BC–AD 100*. Philadelphia: Westminster Press.

Sachs, Hans. (1942). *The Creative Unconscious: Studies in the Psychoanalysis of Art*. Cambridge: Sci-Art Publishers.

Sagan, Eli. (1988). *Freud, Women, and Morality: The Psychology of Good and Evil*. New York: Basic Books.

Sandler, Joseph. (1960). On the concept of the superego. *Psychoanalytic Study of the Child* 15:128–62. Reprinted in: *From Safety to the Superego: Selected Papers of Joseph Sandler*. New York & London: Guilford Press, 1987, pp. 17–44.

———. (1981). Character traits and object relationships. *Psychoanalytic Quarterly* 50:694–708.

Sandler, Joseph, with Freud, Anna. (1985). *The Analysis of Defense: The Ego and the Mechanisms of Defense Revisited*. New York: International Universities Press.

Sandler, Joseph & Rosenblatt, Bernard. (1962). The concept of the representational world. *Psychoanalytic Study of the Child* 17:128–45.

Sarbin, Theodore R. (1950). Contributions to role-taking theory: I. Hypnotic behavior. *Psychological Review* 57(5):255–70.

Sawyier, Fay Horton. (1975). A conceptual analysis of empathy. *Annual of Psychoanalysis* 3:37–47.

Schachtel, Ernest G. (1959). *Metamorphosis: On the Development of Affect, Perception, Attention, and Memory.* New York: Basic Books.

Schafer, Roy. (1959). Generative empathy in the treatment situation. *Psychoanalytic Quarterly* 28:342–73.

———. (1968). *Aspects of Internalization.* Madison, CT: International Universities Press.

Schilder, Paul & Kauders, Otto. (1926). A textbook of hypnosis. In: Paul Schilder. *The Nature of Hypnosis.* Trans. Gerda Corvin. New York: International Universities Press, 1956.

Segal, Hanna. (1952). A psycho-analytical approach to aesthetics. *International Journal of Psycho-Analysis* 33:196–207.

———. (1991). *Dream, Phantasy and Art.* London: Tavistock/Routledge.

Serota, H. M. (1976). Ethics, moral values and psychological interventions: Opening remarks. *International Review of Psycho-Analysis* 3:373–75.

Settlage, Calvin F. (1993). Therapeutic process and developmental process in the restructuring of object and self constancy. *Journal of the American Psychoanalytic Association* 41(2):473–92.

Shainess, Natalie. (1989). The roots of creativity. *American Journal of Psychoanalysis* 49(2):127–38.

Shapiro, Theodore. (1974). The development and distortions of empathy. *Psychoanalytic Quarterly* 43:4–25.

Sharpe, Ella Freeman. (1937). *Dream Analysis: A Practical Handbook for Psycho-Analysts.* London: Hogarth Press; reprinted New York: Brunner/Mazel, 1978.

Shaw, Geraldine A. & Belmore, Susan M. (1982–83). The relation between imagery and creativity. *Imagination, Cognition and Personality* 2:115–23.

Silberer, Herbert. (1909). Report on a method of eliciting and observing certain symbolic hallucination-phenomena. In: David Rapaport (Ed.),

Organization and Pathology of Thought: Selected Sources. New York: Columbia University Press, 1951, pp. 195–207.

———. (1912). On symbol-formation. In: *Organization and Pathology of Thought*, pp. 208–333.

———. ([1918] 1955). The dream: Introduction to the psychology of dreams, trans. Jacob Blauner. *Psychoanalytic Review* 42:361–87.

Silverman, Lloyd H. (1978). Unconscious symbiotic fantasy: A ubiquitous therapeutic agent. *International Journal of Psycho-Analytic Psychotherapy* 7:562–85.

———. (1979). The unconscious fantasy as therapeutic agent in psychoanalytic treatment. *Journal of the American Academy of Psychoanalysis* 7(2):189–218.

Silverman, Lloyd H., Lachmann, Frank M., & Milich, Robert H. (1982). *The Search for Oneness.* New York: International Universities Press.

Sinnott, Edward W. (1959). The creativeness of life. In: Harold H. Anderson (Ed.), *Creativity and Its Cultivation.* New York: Harper & Brothers, pp. 12–29.

Slochower, Harry. (1965). Symbolism and the creative process of art. *American Imago* 22:112–27.

Snyder, Frederick. (1966). Toward an evolutionary theory of dreaming. *American Journal of Psychiatry* 123(2):121–42.

———. (1967). Phenomenology of REM dreaming. APSS abstract. Presented at APSS meeting, Santa Monica.

Solnit, Albert J. (1982). Developmental perspectives on self and object constancy. *Psychoanalytic Study of the Child* 37:201–18.

Sonnenfeld-Schiller, Ludwig. (1972). Psychoanalytic observations on the creative spells of a young scientist. *Israel Annals of Psychiatry and Related Disciplines* 10(2):123–36.

Spanjaard, Jacob. (1969). The manifest dream content and its significance for the interpretation of dreams. *International Journal of Psycho-Analysis* 50:221–35.

Spiro, Melford E. (1993). Tropes, defenses, and unconscious mental representation: Some critical reflections on the "primary process". *Psychoanalysis and Contemporary Thought* 16:155–96.

Stein, Martin H. (1965). States of consciousness in the analytic situation: Including a note on the traumatic dream. In: Max Schur (Ed.), *Drives,*

Affects, Behavior. Vol. 2. Essays in Memory of Marie Bonaparte. New York: International Universities Press, pp. 60–87.

———. (1989). How dreams are told: Secondary revision—The critic, the editor, and the plagiarist. *Journal of the American Psychoanalytic Association* 37/1:65–88.

Sterba, Richard. (1934). The fate of the ego in analytic therapy. *International Journal of Psycho-Analysis* 15(2–3):117–26.

Stern, Daniel N. (1983). The early development of schemas of self, other, and "self with other." In: Joseph D. Lichtenberg & Samuel Kaplan (Eds.), *Reflections on Self Psychology.* Hillsdale, NJ: Analytic Press, pp. 49–84.

———. (1985). *The Interpersonal World of the Infant: A View from Psychoanalysis and Developmental Psychology.* New York: BasicBooks/HarperCollins.

Stewart, Walter A. (1967). Comments on the manifest content of certain types of unusual dreams. *Psychoanalytic Quarterly* 36:329–41.

Stotland, Ezra, Mathews, Jr., Kenneth E., Sherman, Stanley E., Hansson, Robert O., & Richardson, Barbara Z. (1978). *Empathy, Fantasy and Helping.* Beverly Hills: Sage Publications.

Strachey, James. (1934). The nature of the therapeutic action of psychoanalysis. *International Journal of Psycho-Analysis* 15:127–59.

———. (1937). Symposium on the theory of the therapeutic results of psycho-analysis. *International Journal of Psycho-Analysis* 18(2–3):139–45.

Sutherland, J. D. (1963). Object-relations theory and the conceptual model of psychoanalysis. *British Journal of Medical Psychology* 36:109–24.

Tauber, Edward S. & Green, Maurice R. (1959). *Prelogical Experience: An Inquiry into Dreams and Other Creative Processes.* New York: Basic Books.

Thomas, Owen. (1969). *Metaphor: and Related Subjects.* New York: Random House.

Ticho, Ernst A. (1972). The development of superego autonomy. *Psychoanalytic Review* 59:217–33.

Trosman, Harry. (1969). Discussion. In: Milton Kramer, with Roy M. Whitman, Bill J. Baldridge, & Paul H. Ornstein (Eds.), *Dream Psy-*

chology and the New Biology of Dreaming. Springfield, IL: Charles C. Thomas, pp. 57–60.

Tyson, Phyllis (reporter). (1985). Perspectives on the superego. *Journal of the American Psychoanalytic Association* 33:217–31.

Tyson, Phyllis & Tyson, Robert L. (1990). *Psychoanalytic Theories of Development: An Integration.* New Haven: Yale University Press.

Ullman, Montague. (1959). The adaptive significance of the dream. *Journal of Nervous and Mental Diseases* 129:144–49.

———. (1961). Dreaming, altered states of consciousness and the problem of vigilance. *Journal of Nervous and Mental Diseases* 133:529–35.

———. (1969). Dreaming as metaphor in motion. *Archives of General Psychiatry* 21:696–703.

Underhill, Evelyn. (1910). *Mysticism: A Study in the Nature and Development of Man's Spiritual Consciousness.* Reprinted New York: New American Library, Inc, 1955.

Vinacke, William Edgar. (1952). *The Psychology of Thinking.* New York: McGraw-Hill.

Waelder, Robert. (1937). The problem of the genesis of psychical conflict in earliest infancy. *International Journal of Psycho-Analysis* 38:406–73.

Walkup, Lewis E. (1965). Creativity in science through visualization. *Perceptual and Motor Skills* 21:35–41.

Wallach, Michael A. & Wallach, Lise. (1983). *Psychology's Sanction for Selfishness: The Error of Egoism in Theory and Therapy.* San Francisco: W. H. Freeman.

Wallas, Joseph. (1926). *The Art of Thought.* New York: Harcourt, Brace.

Wallwork, Ernest. (1991). *Psychoanalysis and Ethics.* New Haven: Yale University Press.

Ward, Clyde H. (1961). Some further thoughts on the examination dream. *Psychiatry* 24:324–36.

Weiss, Eduardo. (1952). History of metapsychological concepts. In: Franz Alexander & Helen Ross (Eds.), *Dynamic Psychiatry.* Chicago: University of Chicago Press, pp. 40–62.

Weissman, Philip. (1961). Development and creativity in the actor and playwright. *Psychoanalytic Quarterly* 30:549–67.

———. (1967). Theoretical considerations of ego regression and ego functions in creativity. *Psychoanalytic Quarterly* 36:37–51.

———. (1969). Creative fantasies and beyond the reality principle. *Psychoanalytic Quarterly* 38:110–23.

———. (1971). The superego in creative lives and work. *Israel Annals of Psychiatry and Related Disciplines* 9:208–18.

Wheelwright, P. (1962). *Metaphor and Reality*. Bloomington: Indiana University Press.

Whitman, Roy M., Kramer, Milton, Ornstein, Paul H., & Baldridge, Bill J. (1967). The physiology, psychology, and utilization of dreams. *American Journal of Psychiatry* 124(3):43–58.

Winnicott, Donald W. (1953). Transitional objects and transitional phenomena: A study of the first not-me possession. *International Journal of Psycho-Analysis* 34:89–97.

———. (1958). The capacity to be alone. *International Journal of Psycho-Analysis* 39:416–20. Reprinted in: *The Maturational Processes and the Facilitating Environment: Studies in the Theory of Emotional Development*. New York: International Universities Press, 1963, pp. 29–36.

———. (1960a). Comments on "On the concept of the superego": Delivered at a Scientific Meeting of the British Psycho-Analytical Society, 7 December 1960. In: *Psycho-Analytic Explorations*, eds. Clare Winnicott, Ray Shepherd & Madeleine Davis. Cambridge: Harvard University Press, 1989, pp. 465–73.

———. (1960b). The theory of the parent-infant relationship. *International Journal of Psycho-Analysis* 41:585–95. Reprinted in: *The Maturational Processes and the Facilitating Environment*, pp. 37–55.

———. (1963). Communicating and not communicating leading to a study of certain opposites. Reprinted in *The Maturational Processes and the Facilitating Environment*, pp. 179–92.

———. (1966). The location of cultural experience. *International Journal of Psycho-Analysis* 48:368–72.

———. (1971). *Playing and Reality*. London: Tavistock Publications; reprinted Harmondsworth: Penguin Books, 1974.

Wolff, Werner. (1952). *The Dream—Mirror of Conscience. A History of Dream Interpretation from 2000 B.C. and a New Theory of Dream Synthesis*. New York: Grune & Stratton.

Wolfson, Harry Austryn. (1935). The internal senses in Latin, Arabic, and Hebrew philosophic texts. *Harvard Theological Review* 28(2):69–133.

Wright, Kenneth J. T. (1976). Metaphor and symptom: A study of integration and its failure. *International Review of Psycho-Analysis* 3:97–109.

Yazmajian, Richard V. (1968). Slips of the tongue in dreams. *Psychoanalytic Quarterly* 37:588–95.

Index